THE
Strategic
SCHOOL

 **Leadership for Learning**

Series Editors
Willis D. Hawley and E. Joseph Schneider

Joseph Murphy
Leadership for Literacy: Research-Based Practice, PreK–3

P. Karen Murphy, Patricia A. Alexander
Understanding How Students Learn: A Guide for Instructional Leaders

E. Joseph Schneider, Lara L. Hollenczer
The Principal's Guide to Managing Communication

Kenneth A. Strike
Ethical Leadership in Schools: Creating Community in an Environment of
Accountability

Karen Hawley Miles, Stephen Frank
The Strategic School: Making the Most of People, Time, and Money

Please call our toll-free number (800-818-7243)
or visit our Web site (www.corwinpress.com)
to order individual titles or the entire series.

THE Strategic SCHOOL

Making the Most of People, Time, and Money

Karen Hawley Miles • Stephen Frank

A JOINT PUBLICATION

 **CORWIN PRESS**
A SAGE Company
Thousand Oaks, CA 91320

 LEADERSHIP for LEARNING

 NATIONAL ASSOCIATION of SECONDARY SCHOOL PRINCIPALS

For information:

Corwin Press
A SAGE Company
2455 Teller Road
Thousand Oaks, California 91320
www.corwinpress.com

SAGE India Pvt. Ltd.
B 1/I 1 Mohan Cooperative Industrial Area
Mathura Road, New Delhi 110 044
India

SAGE Ltd.
1 Oliver's Yard
55 City Road
London EC1Y 1SP
United Kingdom

SAGE Asia-Pacific Pte. Ltd.
33 Pekin Street #02-01
Far East Square
Singapore 048763

Printed in the United States of America.

Library of Congress Cataloging-in-Publication Data

Miles, Karen Hawley.
The strategic school : making the most of people, time, and money / Karen Hawley Miles and Stephen Frank; a joint publication with the American Association of School Administrators and the National Association of Secondary School Principals.
    p. cm.—(Leadership for learning)
Includes bibliographical references and index.
ISBN 978-1-4129-0416-2 (cloth)
ISBN 978-1-4129-0417-9 (pbk.)
    1. School management and organization—United States. 2. Educational leadership—United States. I. Frank, Stephen. II. American Association of School Administrators. III. National Association of Secondary School Principals. IV. Title. V. Series.

LB2805.M469 2008
371.200973222   2008004861

This book is printed on acid-free paper.

08   09   10   11   12   10   9   8   7   6   5   4   3   2   1

Acquisitions Editor:	Arnis Burvikovs
Editorial Assistants:	Ena Rosen and Irina Dragut
Production Editor:	Cassandra Margaret Seibel
Copy Editor:	Julie Gwin
Typesetter:	C&M Digitals (P) Ltd.
Proofreader:	Victoria Reed-Castro
Indexer:	Jean Casalegno
Cover Designer:	Rose Storey
Graphic Designer:	Monique Hahn

Contents

Foreword

This book by Karen Miles and Stephen Frank is one of a series edited as part of the Leadership for Learning initiative of the American Association of School Administrators (AASA). Its primary purpose is to provide school-level leaders with support in strategic allocation of limited resources to maximize student performance and foster continuous school improvement.

Miles and Frank address a challenge virtually all school leaders confront: How can scarce resources be allocated to enhance the learning of all students? The authors' practical and reliable counsel builds on an artful blend of research on schools and lessons learned from their work with businesses and numerous school districts.

The authors acknowledge that more resources can sometimes increase productivity. But, they argue that what counts most is how resources are used. Thus, school leaders must determine whether the resources they have, which may be all they are likely to get anyway, are used to attain the school's *priority* goals.

It follows that the development of consensus around a limited number of goals for student learning (not goals to establish new programs or processes) is the first step in the strategic allocation of resources. Miles and Frank discuss how this can be done. They go on to focus on how professional expertise, time, and then money can be used strategically. The authors argue that if a school or district wants to substantially increase students' learning, they must invest in what they dub "the Big Three": improving teaching quality, maximizing and targeting academic time, and creating individual attention.

All too often, school resources are allocated in piecemeal and incremental ways, separately from academic planning and prioritization, with ineffective and inefficient results. Among the important lessons emphasized in this book is that it is coherence among the "Big Three" types of initiatives that accelerates and sustains school improvement.

While practical and full of powerful tools for decision making, this is not a prescriptive manual. Miles and Frank recognize that school context, student needs, and existing teacher capacity significantly influence the efficacy of any given improvement strategy. For that reason, they provide a set of research-based principles to guide action that will be productive in all schools.

Willis D. Hawley
E. Joseph Schneider

Preface

THE MOST IMPORTANT QUESTIONS

School leaders enter the education profession because they dream of touching children's lives and building a love of learning, not creating budgets or strategic plans. So, a book on school budgets and resources might not be the passionate educator's choice for bedtime reading. However, we hope this one will make the list, because the link between resource use and student performance may be the key to realizing those dreams that brought us here in the first place.

This relationship between school spending, organization, and student achievement is one of the most unexplored and untested areas of education. Across the country, from one very different community to the next, school budgets and organizations look remarkably similar. When school budget time comes around, most district and school leaders make minor adjustments to the previous year's budget, hoping to preserve existing positions and perhaps purchase some new instructional materials. Most districts use separate processes for budgeting and school planning. Both tend to be unimaginative and routine efforts enacted against the backdrop of looming deadlines, in ways that leave little room for reflecting on or rethinking current practice to help students reach the hopes we have for them.

But what if the budget season were a time for dreams and visions? What kind of schools would we imagine for our own children and for the talented teachers in them? When we ask teachers and principals this question, they get wistful. Elementary school teachers speak of class sizes as small as 15 and time to sit cross-legged on the floor, listening to each child read aloud. Secondary school teachers wish for the opportunity to know their students, to enjoy teaching loads lower than 50 (instead of the current 125-plus), and to spend time working deeply with students on their writing. Both groups envision expert help diagnosing assessment data and hours during the school day to work with other teachers to learn and plan how to adjust their instruction so they challenge each student to his or her limit.

Too often, budget discussions end with the conclusion that there is just not enough money and a clamor for more. Perversely, as important as more resources can be, this response perpetuates the problem. The quest for increased funding implies that if schools did more of what they are already doing, somehow more students would read at grade level and excellent schools would be the norm instead of the widely heralded exception, and that the primary problem lies in the level of funding and not in the nature of how schools are organized.

This book shows how strategic schools have realized these seemingly impossible dreams by reprioritizing and reorganizing their existing resources—people, time, and money. It aims to help school leaders, and the district leaders and policy makers who support them, grapple with a different question. Instead of "How do schools get more?" we ask, "How can schools best use what they already have?" This second question challenges leaders and policy makers to manage resources strategically, be explicit about their priorities for student learning, and reorganize to meet those priorities. It asks school leaders to look closely at their current use of resources first. Adding new resources on top of the old without understanding the answers to these questions ignores evidence that schools can and do improve performance when they prioritize their goals and restructure their resources to match them. Until we rethink the use and organization of resources, we perpetuate a system that does not always serve our purposes very well.

THE NEED FOR COURAGE AND PERSISTENCE

Reorganizing school resources around instructional priorities to transform student performance requires a kind of courage and persistence of will that is hard to muster and harder to sustain. We say "courage" because the primary resource in schools and school districts is people—mostly teachers. So any significant change in the use of resources means teacher and other staff jobs *will* be affected. Using school resources more effectively takes courage because it means setting priorities and being strong enough to say that some things are simply more important than others—even when these priorities demand ending a cherished program. As the examples in this book show, the best choices for children aren't always the favorite options of all of the adults currently working in schools.

Making the most of resources takes courage because it requires schools to increase the impact of the teachers and instructional practices that generate better results than others. Doing this typically means expanding opportunities for expert teachers and supporting less accomplished teachers as they improve their practice. But when school leaders acknowledge the expertise of some teachers over others and mandate specific instructional practices, they challenge deeply ingrained school norms of teacher equality and autonomy. Teachers become uncomfortable. Potential conflicts emerge.

Why persistence? Reorganizing resources takes persistence because rethinking the jobs of teaching staff and restructuring the use of time during the school day enables teachers and other staff to play new roles but does not ensure any magical transformation. An expert teacher must now coach his or her peers; another must learn to mentor new teachers. Learning to play new roles takes time. Investing to grow new capacities takes money.

Designing powerful school organizations takes persistence because it is a continuous and never-ending process. Just as improving teachers learn to adjust instructional practice in response to student need, so do highly effective school organizations reinvent themselves through continuous introspection and discussion. As we will discuss, highly effective school leaders are not content to wait until budget time to readjust their use of time and staff; they tinker constantly, and they do not shy away from making enormous reallocations. They find ways to provide intensive support for struggling students, to adjust time to support instructional needs, and to mobilize teachers to address common challenges.

Creative and flexible resource use demands persistence because a host of regulations, contractual provisions, and district practices combine to thwart changes in school organization. For example, the improved organization might call for the replacement of instructional aide positions with expert reading teachers or perhaps for the purchase of new instructional materials for each classroom. In most districts, these moves would require negotiation with the union, the human resources department, and the budget department. They might have to mount a challenge to legal, policy, and cultural barriers against stout resistance or apathy.

Finally, improving school organization takes persistence because deep changes in instructional practice rarely lead to immediate leaps in standardized test scores. Detractors of change efforts often use this lag between implementation and performance improvement to insist that a school reinstate more familiar routines and structures. It takes both courage and persistence to stay the course.

Finding ways to design more effective school organizations will demand more than school leaders can accomplish on their own. Funding levels, union regulations, and state and district regulations and policies combine with traditional conceptions of what schools should look like to limit the design options available to school leaders. Concerted effort to change the systems that surround and regulate public schools must accompany the deep school-level work we describe here. In this book, we focus on school designs, hoping that the tremendous successes of these strategic-minded, resource-savvy schools will inspire school leaders, teachers, and parents to lobby, push, goad, exhort, and otherwise impel the changes that may be required to create a strategic school.

OBJECTIVES AND ORGANIZATION OF THE BOOK

Together with our colleagues at Education Resource Strategies, the authors have worked for more than 15 years with leaders of public schools to diagnose their current use of resources, learn together about more effective alternatives, and help them choose new and better ways of organizing their people, time, and money. We have enjoyed support from numerous foundations and have analyzed resource use in high- and underperforming schools across the United States. These experiences have convinced us that there is no one right way to organize a school. On the other hand, we find that successful schools share many of the same strategies for organizing people, time, and money in their schools.

The purpose of this book is to provide school leaders and the administrators who support them with a deep understanding of how strategic schools leverage their available people, time, and money to impact student learning. We share both our research—extensive reviews of the literature, in-depth case studies, and district analysis—and our experience in partnering with urban schools and districts across the country to give readers both the academic and practical support they need to make strategic resource decisions in their own schools.

We hope that readers use this book in an active way—rather than skimming it quickly beginning to end. We intend for principals and other school leaders to use this as their own workbook, highlighting ideas that are applicable to their school, entering their own school data into the worksheets and tools provided, and scribbling concrete strategies that could be adapted or implemented in their own school. This book is meant to not only answer the question "What does research say about strategically using people, time, and money to improve learning?" but to also answer the follow-up question—"and how do I get started in my school?" This book is meant to be a tool for change.

The remainder of the book is organized into three parts:

- Part I: The "Big Three" Guiding Resource Strategies
- Part II: How Strategic Schools Use People, Time, and Money
- Part III: How to Make the Most of Your School's People, Time, and Money

In Part I, we make the case for more strategic use of school resources to fit our new goals and learning technologies. We outline a brief history of how and why resources have come to be poorly organized in typical American schools; why it is imperative for schools to reexamine and reconsider how they use the people, time, and money they already receive; and why now is a good time to get started. We also describe a gap in the body of research on successful schools as it relates to providing guidance for how schools might best organize and allocate resources—a gap this book aims to begin to fill.

At the end of the first section, we introduce the framework that will be used throughout the rest of the book. First, we introduce the "Big Three" guiding resource strategies that describe how the strategic schools we have studied organize their people, time, and money. These strategic schools are schools that achieved high performance by purposefully allocating their resources to better meet their biggest needs.

Part II dives more deeply into each of the Big Three guiding resource strategies. In each chapter, we describe each strategy, chart key differences between typical and strategic schools, and discuss why these differences matter. We also present case examples that illustrate how each principle contributed to the success of one or more strategic schools.

Part III is the practical application section of the book and deserves special mention here because we hope that users will stop, gather some information about their school, and then use the framework to develop a resource strategy that meets their school's particular needs.

Chapter 6, "Tools for Strategic Schools: How Well Does Your School Use People, Time, and Money?" uses a case example to walk readers through the process of inventorying current resource use and considering strategies for reallocation. This chapter includes three practical tools to record your school's resource data and evaluate whether your school follows the principles outlined in Part II.

Chapters 7 through 9 are designed to guide the reader through three interrelated planning processes that are essential to creating a strategic school plan:

- How to group students and assign teachers (Chapter 7)
- How to craft a master schedule that works (Chapter 8)
- How to strategically improve teaching quality (Chapter 9)

The three processes described in these chapters are so interrelated that decisions in one chapter will invariably affect decisions reached in other chapters. Chapter 10, "Putting It All Together," will challenge the reader to integrate the various aspects of the strategic planning process to create a schedule, staffing plan, professional development plan, and student assignment policy that work together to meet a school's needs.

In this book, we focus on the school as the center point for effective resource use while being very clear that schools operate within a larger system that can either facilitate or seriously frustrate strategic resource allocation. We begin here not because districts and states shouldn't rethink their paradigms and practices, but because those who work to support schools need to have a clear vision of what they are trying to enable—strategic resource use that leads to student success—and that begins from the school up. With this vision in mind, reformers and district leaders can more effectively identify what needs to change to better support strategic school resource use. Whenever possible, we at Education Resource Strategies work with school leaders at the same time as we work with district leaders, believing that revolution must happen from the bottom up and the top down at once.

Acknowledgments

W e want to thank the teachers, principals, and central office staff in our partner schools and districts for allowing us to study and learn from the critical work you do to support student success. The insight gained from these partnerships serves as the backbone for this book, and we are grateful to the practitioners who shared their experiences as they worked to use resources more strategically to bolster student learning.

We also want to thank the entire Education Resource Strategies team for your dedication, insight, and perseverance as we work to gain a deeper understanding of strategic resource use. In particular, thank you to Regis Shields for constantly challenging and improving the text and to our faithful editor, Simmons Lettre, for shepherding this book through the writing process and keeping us smiling throughout.

We are grateful to our anonymous reviewers for your helpful comments, which improved this text and made it even more relevant and useful for the practitioners reading this book. We want to thank Willis Hawley for his always-thoughtful comments and rigorous editing and for encouraging us to persevere in creating our vision of strategic schools. We also appreciate the support of The Bill & Melinda Gates Foundation, which provided funding for most of the high school case studies included in this book.

Finally, thank you to those who have encouraged us to study and develop our ideas further. Your support and faith continue to push us to learn more and become better at supporting others in using our findings to improve learning for students.

PUBLISHER'S ACKNOWLEDGMENTS

Corwin Press gratefully acknowledges the contributions of the following reviewers:

Sue Belish
Superintendent
Sheridan County School District #1
Ranchester, WY

Stephen Handley
Superintendent
Hinds County School District
Raymond, MS

Douglas Gordon Hesbol
Superintendent
Laraway CCSD 70C
Joliet, IL

Tricia Peña
Principal
Cienega High School
Vail, AZ

Dana Salles Trevethan
Principal
Turlock High School
Turlock, CA

About the Authors

**Karen Hawley Miles** is executive director and founder of Education Resource Strategies, a nonprofit organization in Boston, Massachusetts, that specializes in strategic planning, organization, and resource allocation in urban public school districts. Her work aims to help states, districts, and schools rethink resource allocation and use to empower principals to create great schools and redirect resources to promote excellent teaching, individual attention for children, and productive instructional time. Dr. Miles has worked intensively with urban districts like Los Angeles, Chicago, Albuquerque, Boston, Baltimore, Providence, Rochester, and Cincinnati to deeply analyze and improve their funding systems, school-level resource use, and investment in professional development. She has taught school leaders at Harvard University, in school districts, with New Leaders for New Schools, and with the Broad Institute for School Boards. Currently, she directs a multiyear project funded by the Gates Foundation to understand the costs and organization of small, high-performing high schools and help districts organize to better support them. Prior to her work at Education Resource Strategies, she worked at Bain & Company as a strategy and management consultant for hospitals and corporations. She has a BA in economics from Yale University and a doctorate in education from Harvard University, specializing in school organization, change, and finance.

**Stephen Frank** is the cofounder of Education Resource Strategies, a nonprofit corporation that works with urban superintendents across the country to improve student performance through a more effective use of resources. Client school systems include New York City, Los Angeles, Chicago, Atlanta, the District of Columbia, Baltimore, Rochester, Albuquerque, and Oakland, among others. Dr. Frank

has helped create strategic leadership training programs and tools that have been used in principal training programs across the country. He specializes in helping school systems better measure how funds travel through school systems; how schools actually use the time, people, and money they receive; and how school system processes must change to improve student performance through better resource use. He has written and presented on these subjects extensively. Prior to co-founding Education Resource Strategies, Dr. Frank worked for Bain & Company, a global strategy consulting firm; taught at the Terry Sanford Institute of Public Policy at Duke University; and founded and ran a private language school. He is a former Fulbright Fellow and lives in the Dallas–Fort Worth metropolitan area, where his three children attend public school.

PART I

The "Big Three" Guiding Resource Strategies

Why Rethink School Resources Now?

1

A s we move into the new millennium, education is at the top of the public agenda. Americans look to schooling as an investment in the future. We insist that schools help our children meet higher, more clearly defined standards so that they will be prepared for a high-technology world we can only begin to imagine. The ability to quantify student performance more accurately has heightened attention on ensuring that students in high poverty and from different backgrounds are not left behind in the Information Age. We expect schools to do for all children what only the best schools and most capable teachers have done for some in the past. These goals, which focus on all children mastering standards, are different from the ones schools were organized to meet.

In the past, schools aimed to cover content material and paid much less attention to what children learned and who learned it. Today's challenging goals change the job of teaching and the needs for resources. Significant new resources have been added over this time period that might allow new models of instruction and schooling, yet the basic organization of schools has remained stubbornly unchanging for the past 50 years. Throughout this book, we argue that although new resources may ultimately be required, we must first rethink the basic structures and patterns of school organization to free existing resources for more flexible student- and teacher-oriented models of schooling.

NEW GOALS REQUIRE NEW WAYS OF WORKING

Historically, school organizations were never set up to guarantee student *learning.* Instead, schools originally intended to socialize children and to provide students *access* to certain knowledge and skills (Tyack & Cuban,

1995). The basic structures of modern public schools—the collections of classrooms organized by age and subject, teacher salary schedules, and district administration—were created to ensure exposure to ideas and skills (Darling Hammond, 2001). As Figure 1.1 illustrates, instead of measuring what students could do, districts were set up to measure credits received and material covered. Rather than checking whether teachers were actually helping students gain new knowledge, they required that teachers cover a specified curriculum. When some students struggled and fell behind, the system treated this as a natural outcome of innate differences in ability. These organizational features are so consistent that Tyack and Tobin (1994) called them the "grammar of schooling" and Sarason (1971/1982) the "regularities."

Figure 1.1   Comparison of old goals for schools to new goals for schools

From Schools . . .	→	To Schools . . .
Presenting subject matter	→	Ensuring students learn subject matter content
Sorting students: the "elite" reach highest standards	→	Helping all students meet rigorous academic standards
Preparing students for predictable jobs	→	Preparing students for a rapidly changing workplace with emphasis on literacy and critical thinking skills

Not surprisingly, this organization of resources has resulted in some students achieving at high levels, but also in significant gaps between students who succeed and those who don't. According to national tests from 2003, 37% of fourth graders, 26% of eighth graders, and 26% of twelfth graders are reading below the basic level (see Figure 1.2). The basic level indicates a "partial mastery of prerequisite knowledge and skills that are fundamental to proficient work at each grade" (U.S. Department of Education, National Center for Education Statistics [NCES], 2003). A large percentage of students also write below the basic level: 14% of fourth graders, 15% of eighth graders, and 26% of twelfth graders.

Focusing on urban students, a strikingly large percentage of students in large urban districts cannot read and write at or above proficient levels. Nationwide, only 36% of urban fourth graders scored at or above proficient levels in reading, and by eighth grade, only one third scored at the proficient level or above. In 2002, only 13% of Washington, DC, and Los Angeles fourth-grade students scored at or above proficient levels in reading and only 10% in writing (U.S. Department of Education, NCES, 2003).

Figure 1.2   U.S. student scores on the 2003 National Assessment of
                   Educational Progress

Grade Level	Reading		Writing	
	Below Basic	At or Above Basic	Below Basic	At or Above Basic
Grade 4	37	63	14	86
Grade 8	26	74	15	85
Grade 12	26 (2002)	74 (2002)	26	74

SOURCE: U.S. Department of Education, National Center for Education Statistics (2003).

The responses of standards-based reform and school accountability embody different ideas that require new educational strategies. To teach students instead of material, schools must regularly diagnose what students know, what they can do, and what they may have missed. To teach *all* students, teachers must adopt instructional strategies that fit each student's individual needs and find ways to respond to students who haven't yet grasped the material. Time spent on subjects and skills must vary based on how long it takes students to master them rather than moving in lock-step according to schedule.

To accomplish standards-driven goals, teachers must work together in new ways. When the only concern was covering curriculum, teachers could work independently, because they didn't need to know or build on what students actually learned. Now, the most sophisticated tests measure students' cumulative knowledge of curriculum material. This means that schools must consciously organize to create continuity over time and to adjust to students' different backgrounds, paces, and learning styles. Regardless of their subject, specialty, or training, teachers are now held collectively responsible for developing their students' literacy and problem-solving skills. Clearly, new goals require new instructional strategies and thus a fundamental rethinking of how to organize resources to accomplish them.

TRIPLING OF SPENDING LEVELS, BUT LITTLE
CHANGE IN CORE STRUCTURES OF SCHOOLING

Responding to the gap between old structures and our new, higher goals for schools may eventually require that society devote more resources to education. But first, it makes sense to diagnose the current investment. Nationwide, spending on each student, adjusted for inflation, roughly tripled between 1960 and the end of the millennium. It rose from an average of $2,100 to slightly more than $6,900 in 1999 (U.S. Department of Education, NCES, 1999b). About half of this increase came from growth in average salary and compensation levels and the other half from the addition of more staff (Miles, 1997).

Importantly, the fact that average teaching compensation rose does not mean that teacher salaries rose relative to comparable professions. Much of the overall growth in compensation has been driven by the increasing cost of benefits for all employees over the last three decades. Because teacher salary levels rise with teacher experience, the overall rise in teacher tenure also contributes to the rise in average salaries. A 2004 analysis by the Economic Policy Institute that adjusts for time worked, benefits, and seniority suggests that in the last 10 years, teacher salaries have fallen by about 14% compared with those in similarly skilled professions (Allegretto, Corcoran, & Mishel, 2004). Beyond this reduction in wages, the structure of teacher salaries has remained the same since the 1960s across the nation (Miles, 1997).

During this period of increased spending, schools increased the size of their staffs. For example, in 1960, schools averaged one staff person (not counting custodians and lunch workers) for every 17 students; now there is one adult for every 9. In 1960, schools had one teacher for every 27 students; they now average one teacher for every 17 (see Figure 1.3). This student-teacher ratio holds true even for districts with more than 50,000 students (one teacher per 17 students in 1997).

Although the number of teachers has doubled, classroom life for most students and teachers feels much the same because class size has changed very little over the past decades. In 1960, for example, elementary class sizes averaged 28 students. By 1997, that number dropped only to 24. Over the same period at the secondary level, average class sizes did not change meaningfully at all, staying at 26 (see Figure 1.3).

Staff positions have been added largely outside of the regular-education classroom, including staff working with special populations of students such as special-education or bilingual students or as subject specialists like art and music teachers in elementary schools. In 1960, 70% of district staff were teachers. By 1997, barely half, 52%, were teachers (U.S. Department of Education, NCES, 1999a). Over the same period, the proportion of regular classroom teachers dropped even more, from 84% to 39% of the instructional staff (U.S. Department of Education, NCES, 1999a; see Figure 1.4).

Figure 1.3   The basic structure of schooling has remained the same

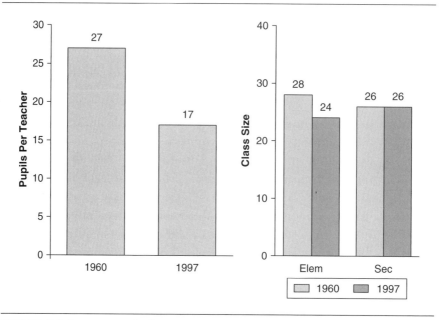

SOURCE: U.S. Department of Education, National Center for Education Statistics (1997).

Figure 1.4   Instructional staff by type, 1960 to 1997

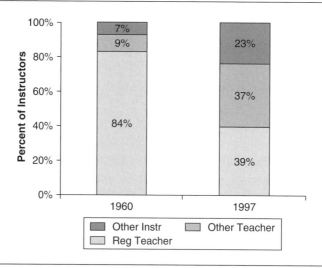

SOURCE: Estimations based on U.S. Department of Education, National Center for Education Studies (1999a), Table 93, and the analysis of Miles (1997).

RESOURCES TIED BY RIGID
STRUCTURES INHIBIT RETHINKING

Based on the previous findings, if schools are receiving increased funds, why are they not producing increased performance? Our research and experience suggests that at least part of the reason is that these additional resources are tied up by outdated and rigid structures, practices, and norms that make it hard for practitioners to redirect resources to best impact student learning.

Perhaps the most important of these sets of structures, practices, and norms surrounds the standard public-school approach for responding to individual learning needs that has evolved over the last half-century. It originated when goals for schooling were different, funding levels lower, regular class sizes much higher, and assessment tools relatively primitive. We call this traditional approach the "cycle of specialization and isolation" (see Figure 1.5). It has been reinforced by the incremental increases to school funding that have been layered onto the old structures. In this paradigm, all students begin in large classrooms with students sorted by age but sometimes very different skill levels. In the context of very large class sizes and limited understanding of how to diagnose, measure, and respond to individual student skill levels and needs, it made logical sense to remove a few students from the regular classroom and provide extra support from specialists who had more time to help them.

Over time, legislation and court rulings began to mandate this practice, while providing only partial funding to do so. Title I, the federal Individuals With Disabilities in Education Act, and other programs provided funding to serve students living in poverty, students with special learning needs, gifted students, and students with limited proficiency in English. However, these funds came with varying levels of stipulations about how to serve these children and what types of professionals were qualified to do so.

These practices add some new resources to schools from the federal government and states, but they have had an astonishing effect. Over the period from 1967 to 1996, spending levels adjusted for inflation doubled to an average of $6,576 per student. However, 58% of the new resources went to support special programs for special populations of students. Only 23% of the new resources supported regular education programming (Rothstein, 1996; Rothstein & Miles, 1995). From 1991 to 1996, spending on special programs actually drained resources from regular education programs. In 1967, 80% of school spending supported regular programs, and by 1996, this had fallen to just over 50%.

Figure 1.5   The cycle of specialization and isolation

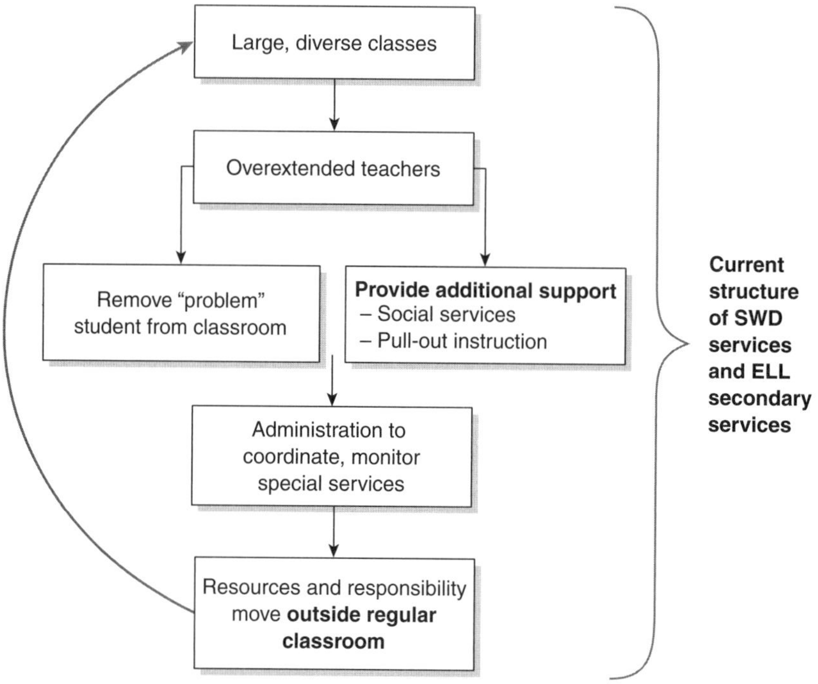

NOTE: SWD = students with disabilities; ELL = English language learners.

Thus, the cycle continues and intensifies. The practice of providing isolated, specialized services drains dollars from other students and teachers and creates incentives to categorize or overdiagnose students as having special needs. In some cases, it can also diffuse responsibility for the neediest students as they may leave their homeroom to work with other teachers during literacy or math time. Some consider this type of disruption damaging (Oakes, 1989; Tyack & Cuban, 1995).

In summary, the old goals for schools led to organizational structures that have now become accepted as the way schools work. As Figure 1.6 shows, the organizational practices or structures that exert the most impact include the structure of teacher jobs and salaries; the practice of age-graded, subject-specific classes with set sizes that vary little by subject or grade; the unstrategic use of time; and the practice of pulling students out of the mainstream when they do not meet expectations. These structures are reinforced by local and state funding levels, staffing practices, union contracts, and even state laws stipulating everything from class size to teacher salary levels. Even though the goals have changed, along with our understanding of how to meet them, these rigid structures make it hard, but not impossible, for principals to rethink the way they use their people, time, and money.

Figure 1.6 Old goals link to rigid structures that inhibit rethinking of resources

Old Goals for Students . . .	Led to "The Way Schools Work"	Resulting Organizational Practices That Inhibit Rethinking Resources
Present subject matter.	Teachers work independently and do not know or build on what students actually learned. This teacher autonomy also leads to no individual or joint responsibility for results. Teacher subject knowledge valued, but there is no reward for results.	Teachers work in isolation without meaningful common time to collaborate with each other during the student day. Teacher salary structures rise with experience and course taking instead of student learning and role. Teaching career doesn't include leadership opportunities.
Provide access to subject matter, but do not guarantee student learning.	Students in standard class sizes, individual attention not critical because no systematic attempt is made to ensure learning for all.	Schools use formulas to govern class and group sizes.
	Grade-level curriculum dominates the school.	Students move through school based on age, not mastery of curriculum.
	Teachers spend time in the same way each day to cover the various curriculum materials. The school year always moves in increments of 180 days.	Unstrategic lock-step scheduling of student time, especially at the secondary school level, is not linked to curriculum and educational needs.
Sort students: The "elite" reach highest standards.	Students who fall behind are put into remedial programs, lower tracks, or special programs.	Schools use "pull-out" or tracking practices to respond to individual needs, resulting in a high percentage of specialized personnel to address individual learning needs.
Prepare students for predictable jobs.	Emphasis is on learning a defined body of knowledge or specific career-related skills instead of developing critical thinking skills.	

REASONS FOR OPTIMISM

Although many schools feel bound or limited by historically evolved structures, we increasingly find that the climate is right for new thinking. Although rethinking resources to create new kinds of school organizations will require challenging many of the deeply ingrained and virtually uniform organizational practices of schools across the country, there are also forces working to make school reform easier.

First, the current accountability movement associated with No Child Left Behind is building public demand for school success. Clearer measurement and wide reporting of student results has heightened public dissatisfaction and is pushing school leaders to search for support in areas previously overlooked, including resource use. The call for greater efficiency naturally suggests a hard look at resource use and provides an entry point for rethinking strategies in this area.

Second, federal, state, and district administrators are also easing restrictions on how schools use and organize funds. Title I provisions now allow schools to apply their federal funds across the entire school program if poverty levels reach threshold levels. States from California to Massachusetts are looking to combine funding sources into block grants that allow more integrated use of funds. Districts around the country, such as Oakland, Cincinnati, Seattle, and Houston, are pushing more resources to schools and allowing more flexible use, or even allocating resources as dollars instead of as specific staff positions. Third, research linking student performance to resource use is being spurred by better data on student performance and resource use, and by an explosion of alternative school designs. The growth in charter schools and small high schools that operate (in some cases) with fewer resource constraints will continue to generate more variation in spending patterns and organization, providing a richer source of information to test ideas about the cost effectiveness of reforms.

Finally, resources are on the minds of school leaders across the country. Budgets and resource allocation are increasingly a focal point of discourse on school improvement. A spate of state lawsuits have focused attention on the question of how much it takes to educate students with different levels of needs and how to ensure that all school districts have enough. A landmark case in New York State awarded an additional $6 billion dollars along with increased instructional time to students in the state. Other reformers focus on specific aspects of resource use. The widely promoted "65% solution" seeks to legislate that school districts devote 65% of all resources to instruction (see www.firstclasseducation.org). The nonprofit group Massachusetts 2020 is creating a first-in-the-nation effort to allow multiple school districts to expand the school day and year. Supported financially by the Massachusetts legislature and U.S. Department of Education, schools apply for planning and implementation grants to add two hours to their school day and increase time in core academics, enrichment, teacher planning, and professional development (see www .mass2020.org).

These factors are beginning to make it easier for schools to rethink the way they organize to improve student success. We shall see that the successful schools we highlight did not transform themselves by making marginal refinements to existing budgets in the context of legacy structures. Instead, they overcame this legacy by creatively reorganizing their schedules, professional development plans, staffing strategies, and student assignment policies. They reorganized the people, time, and money in their schools to better match their priorities. They became strategic schools.

How Do Resources **2** Matter?

Against all odds, some schools consistently manage to outperform others that have similar challenges and student populations. The obvious question is why? What makes these outstanding schools tick? Why do they succeed where others fail?

The answer to this question is encouraging. Decades-long research on effective schools has been so consistent in its findings that a general consensus around the characteristics of higher-performing schools has emerged (Edmonds, 1979; Education Trust, 1999; Hawley, 2002; Marzano, 2003; National Association of Secondary School Principals, 2004; Newmann, Smith, Allensworth, & Bryk, 2001; Springboard Schools, 2003; Williams et al., 2005). In recent review of this work, Marzano (2003) grouped them into five key traits as follows:

1. A guaranteed and viable curriculum

2. Challenging goals and effective feedback

3. Parent and community involvement

4. A safe and orderly environment

5. Collegiality and professionalism

District leaders and school reformers have developed a bevy of assessment tools, training programs, and specific school designs that promote these characteristics in schools. The comprehensive school reform movement that began in the 1990s and continues today spurred the creation of school designs (or models) that specify aligned standards, curriculum, and instructional practices as well as a process for implementing these features (Bodilly, 1998; Glennan, 1998). The National Education Association (1990) has built evaluation tools that support a set of six critical characteristics it calls

KEYS to school effectiveness. Importantly, creating these conditions requires schools to reorganize people, time, and money in very different ways than traditionally seen in schools. Despite this, most of these lists scarcely mention the relationship between success and resource redesign. Marzano's (2003) list encompasses many resource decisions without mentioning any resource issues specifically. Meanwhile, the KEYS list, like many others, suggests vaguely that highly effective schools use resources "effectively to support teaching and learning" (Hawley, 2002).

RESEARCH ON RESOURCE USE IS INADEQUATE TO DATE

Although strategic resource use forms the bedrock of effective schools, research on this key factor is inadequate to date for several reasons. First, most research on resources focuses on the relationship between overall spending level and student achievement. Although it is a subject of vigorous academic and political debate, there is no conclusive statistical evidence that when student characteristics are controlled, higher-spending schools get better student performance results (Hanushek, 1997; Hedges, Laine, & Greenwald, 1994; Ladd & Hansen, 1999; Odden, Picus, Goetz, & Fermanich, 2006). It is important to note that there may be threshold levels of spending below which effective schooling is not possible.

In our own research, we also find a weak relationship between spending levels and student achievement. Consider Figure 2.1, in which each point represents a different school in a Texas district we studied recently. Our analysis found that after adjusting for student need, the general-fund dollars per student varied widely across individual schools. This finding is similar to what we find in almost every district we study.

However, as shown in Figure 2.2, after mapping school-level resources to student performance, we see that both high-performing and low-performing schools are found at all funding levels.

Although these findings seem to defy common sense, they are not so surprising when we consider that it matters very much *how* resources are used (Murnane & Levy, 1996).

Scholars have found plenty of evidence to support the importance of rethinking how resources are used. For instance, Odden and Archibald (2001) compared spending and staffing patterns of exceptionally effective schools against the patterns found in other schools across the nation. They examined the percentage of resources spent on broad categories such as instruction, administration, and student support and found that typical schools had strikingly similar patterns. The effective schools, by contrast,

Figure 2.1   General-fund dollars per weighted student*

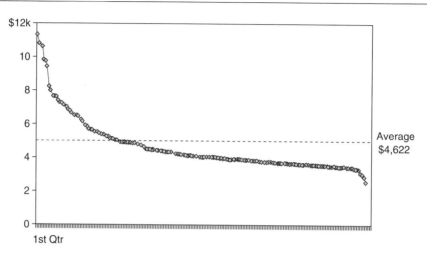

*Students adjusted for poverty, English language learners, and special education

Figure 2.2   The organization and use of resources determines performance

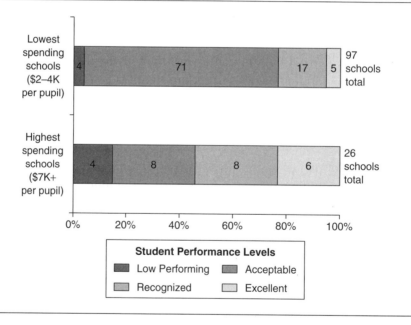

spent a significantly larger portion of their resources on instruction (Odden & Archibald, 2001).

But the percentage of resources spent on instruction is still a fairly gross measure of how schools use resources. Although spending more money on instruction is probably a good idea in many cases, it seems unlikely to be a panacea for all school ills. We need a more nuanced understanding of what high-performing schools are doing with the resources they receive. Unfortunately, statistical research doesn't provide much help.

A large body of quantitative research explores the importance of specific inputs such as teacher education levels, experience, and class size. We will review it in more detail in later chapters. This research clearly suggests that the way schools organize resources matters. However, it doesn't provide much guidance about the relative impact of these different inputs and when they matter most, nor does it come to a consensus on how schools can implement an effective resource strategy. Furthermore, these input-focused studies lack an overarching theory of action about how resources work together to improve student learning.

UNDERSTANDING HOW RESOURCES MATTER DEMANDS A HOLISTIC APPROACH

To generate this understanding of how resources interact and the ways practitioners can most successfully use them to improve performance, researchers need to study how all resources—people, time, and money—work together. Research by Newmann et al. (2001) took this holistic approach by constructing a framework for describing and measuring a notion they called "instructional coherence" in schools. They defined schools with instructional coherence as having three overarching conditions:

- a common instructional framework that guides curriculum, teaching, and assessment;
- staff working conditions that support implementation of the framework, including clear standards, hiring and induction procedures, teacher evaluation, and professional development; and
- allocation of resources such as staff, time, and materials to advance the framework.

Using a combination of survey and teacher observation, these researchers measured the instructional coherence of schools over a three-year period. They compared schools that improved their scores on these three conditions of "coherence" to schools that did not improve their scores. The schools that improved their coherence showed twice as much improvement in student performance.

This finding suggests that schools need an overarching instructional framework and a resource strategy to support it. However, the literature does not provide school leaders with support for how to create a resource strategy that fits each school's unique constellation of student and faculty needs in the context of the school's overall design.

OUR RESEARCH: CASE STUDIES

The remainder of this book seeks to fill this gap between research and practice. We present findings from our own action research as a strategic framework for evaluating resource use in schools. We also provide concrete suggestions on how to develop and implement an effective resource strategy. This research, some of which is presented here for the first time, comes from our experience studying resource use in thousands of schools across the country over the last 15 years. Our research also builds on an extensive survey of the education literature and on our collaboration with some of the field's most prominent scholars, most especially Allan Odden, Sarah Archibald, Mark Fermanich, and Linda Darling-Hammond.

Much of our research relies on case studies. Case studies are particularly effective for studying resource use because they allow us to examine not just one input such as class size, but the interaction between class size and other components of the resource picture, such as teaching quality and use of time. They allow us to study the choices and tradeoffs schools make in the context of their instructional design, student needs, and teacher capacity. While conducting research for this book, we have published numerous case studies on school-level resource use, choosing schools that

- outperformed other schools in their districts or improved student performance dramatically,
- served a student population similar to (or in some cases more needy than) the typical district school,
- had consciously addressed their organization and use of resources as part of their efforts to improve performance,
- received roughly the same level of resources as comparable schools in their city, and
- had been operating for at least four years (Miles & Darling-Hammond, 1997; Shields & Miles, 2008).

Although we allude to many schools in this book, our findings are based primarily on a deep analysis of the case study schools listed in Figure 2.3, which include a diverse range of elementary, middle, and secondary schools. Because each of these schools achieved outstanding success by reorganizing the way they used resources, we refer to them interchangeably as high-performing schools or strategic schools.

Figure 2.3   Strategic schools

School Name	Grade Span	City, State
Elementary Schools		
Dever	K–5	Boston, MA
Douglass	K–5	Memphis, TN
Hurley	K–5	Boston, MA
Mary C. Lyon	K–5	Boston, MA
Mather	K–5	Boston, MA
Quebec Heights	K–6	Cincinnati, OH
Middle Schools		
Clifton Elementary	PreK–8	Cincinnati, OH
Rafael Hernandez	PreK–8	Boston, MA
Graham & Parks	6–8	Cambridge, MA
Central Park East Secondary	7–12	New York, NY
University Park	7–12	Worcester, MA
High Schools		
Academy of the Pacific Rim	9–12	Boston, MA
Boston Arts Academy	9–12	Boston, MA
High Tech High	9–12	San Diego, CA
International High	9–12	New York, NY
Life Academy	9–12	Oakland, CA
Met West	9–12	Oakland, CA
Nobel St. Charter High School	9–12	Chicago, IL
Perspectives Charter	6–12	Chicago, IL
Tech Boston Academy	9–11	Boston, MA

These strategic schools are located throughout the country and have different student populations, school sizes, organizations, infrastructures, and instructional models. Although some of these schools began as innovative schools, others were low-performing schools that achieved transformational performance improvement by rethinking the way they used people, time, and money.

We collected data through visits and interviews, and by gathering and reviewing detailed budgets, improvement plans, and course schedules from each school. We remain convinced that there is no one way to use resources effectively in schools—no set class size that will predictably improve results and no specific amount of time that must be spent. Instead, successful schools employ a common set of strategies and principles as they seek to make most effective use of their resources. These common strategies form the core of the analytic framework presented in this book. Rather than present this book as a summary of cases, we felt it would be more helpful to the reader to interpret the cases and present pieces of each case thematically to illustrate a specific point. Therefore, each case may be referred to in multiple chapters to support different strategic points.

A FRAMEWORK—THE "BIG THREE" GUIDING RESOURCE STRATEGIES AND RESOURCE PRINCIPLES

In analyzing our case study data, we searched for patterns of resource use across schools and found that despite differences in school level, size, location, student population, or even instructional focus, high-performing schools used their resources in very consistent ways. Although their specific strategies varied to reflect differences in context, instructional approach, or staff, each school organized its resources around three guiding resource strategies. Specifically, strategic schools organize and use resources to

- invest to continuously improve teaching quality through hiring, professional development, job structure, and common planning time;
- create individual attention and personal learning environments; and
- use student time strategically by emphasizing core academics and literacy (see Figure 2.4).

We have dubbed these organizing principles the "Big Three" guiding resource strategies (Miles, 2001). Other research both confirms and expands on these guiding resource strategies (Allington & Cunningham, 2002; Darling-Hammond, 2001; Education Trust, 1999; Marzano, 2003; Odden & Archibald, 2001).

As we look across the schools we have studied, we find that although high-performing schools organize their resources to address all of the Big Three strategies, each school does so in its own unique way, depending on its own specific needs. For example, a school staffed with a high percentage of experienced and successful teachers may place more emphasis on

Figure 2.4 "Big Three" guiding resource strategies

creating more individual attention than on revamping its professional development system—a system that is already working well. In contrast, a school with a relatively new and inexperienced teaching staff may emphasize the teaching quality principle more than the other two, perhaps investing less to increase time in core academics and more on improving the teaching in those classes. High-performing schools look at their staff and students first to determine their needs and then create a resource strategy that addresses those specific needs.

Strategic schools implement these strategies by following a series of resource principles, shown in Figure 2.5. These principles further clarify the types of resource use seen in the case study schools and may help practitioners as they try to implement the Big Three in their own schools.

Figure 2.5 "Big Three" guiding resource strategies and principles

1. **Invest in teaching quality through hiring, professional development, job structure, and common planning time by**
   A. Hiring and organizing staff to fit school needs in terms of expertise, philosophy, and schedule
   B. Integrating significant resources for well-designed professional development that provides expert support to implement the school's core instructional design
   C. Designing teacher work schedules to include blocks of collaborative planning time effectively used to improve classroom practice
   D. Enacting systems that promote individual teacher growth through induction, leadership opportunities, professional development planning, evaluation, and compensation

(Continued)

Figure 2.5 (Continued)

2. **Create individual attention and personal learning environments by**

   E. Assessing student learning to adjust instruction and support
   F. Creating smaller group sizes and reducing teacher loads in high-need areas
   G. Organizing structures that foster personal relationships between students and teachers

3. **Use student time strategically, emphasizing core academics and literacy by**

   H. Maximizing time, including longer blocks of uninterrupted time, that students spend on academic subjects
   I. Varying time and instructional programs to ensure all students meet rigorous academic standards

PART II

How Strategic Schools Use People, Time, and Money

Dr. Mary Nash, an administrator in Boston Public Schools, had always considered resources to be financial. While working with her in the district, we met to suggest that she could find the $2 million she needed for a new professional development program by eliminating pullouts in Title I and resource rooms and reallocating the funds to provide professional development to teachers districtwide. As Dr. Nash tells it, during this meeting, "We were polite but thought the idea was really ridiculous. But we decided to check it out, just to make sure." After running the figures with her colleagues, they realized that they could harness the resources and redirect funds in ways that could improve instruction and learning. She comments, "This was the first time I learned that resources are much more than just dollars."

Dr. Nash took this notion and ran with it in ways that we had never seen before. An expert on emotionally disturbed students, Dr. Nash eventually launched and led a highly successful inclusion school, the Mary Lyon School, with classrooms of 15 students each—10 regular-education and 5 emotionally disturbed students. Each classroom is staffed with one master teacher, a paraprofessional, and often an intern. One hundred percent of the students at this school consistently pass the state examinations. Details of Dr. Nash's resource use are included throughout the next two sections, and she believes that the key to using resources effectively is realizing that "how you spend your resources—financial, time, and human—really does speak to the ethics, morals, and values about what is important."

Each of the chapters in this section describes one of the "Big Three" resource strategies and principles, charts key differences between typical and strategic schools, and presents case evidence from one or more of our strategic schools to illustrate each point.

The combination of research and real-world examples is intended to build a strong supporting case for the recommended actions and activities in Part III.

Investing in Teaching Quality

3

THE MOST IMPORTANT CHALLENGE

Principals, parents, and students experience firsthand what research shows—that the quality of teaching trumps any other factor in predicting improved student performance. Research also confirms what any parent who has fought to place their child with the best teacher each year understands—developing successful learners takes more than one good teacher. It takes a school. As intuitive as these premises seem, most schools do not consistently make resource choices that weigh teaching quality over other factors. They do not always invest in or organize to promote the ongoing improvement of instruction.

Instead, schools tend to focus their energy and resources to reduce class sizes, increase instructional time, or enact similar structural changes. Such "improvements" are easier to measure and simpler to implement. But focusing on structural changes can draw attention from the area where long-lasting improvement begins—better instruction through higher teaching capacity.

Research suggests that most schools could benefit from organizing in ways that weight teaching quality over other priorities. For example, studies demonstrate that when faced with the option of lowering class size by a few students or investing to ensure higher teaching quality, the choice is clear. Choosing the more effective teacher leads to more student learning (Halbach, Ehrle, Zahorick, & Molnar, 2001; Rice, 2002a, 2002b). In fact, in one highly regarded analysis, Greenwald, Hedges, and Laine (1996) found that high-quality teaching is about five times more effective than typical reductions in class size. Similarly, small groups, individual tutoring, and increased academic time only have significant benefit on student performance when the quality of instruction is high (Allington & Cunningham, 2002; Berliner, 1979; Wasik & Slavin, 1993).

It takes more than one or even a few teachers to generate the kind of sustained student learning that defies the odds. Rivkin, Hanushek, and

Kane (2000) found that students who have an above-average teacher for three years in a row outperform students who have a below-average teacher for three years by an entire grade level. When teachers feel a collective sense of responsibility for student learning and work together to improve instruction, in other words, when they form professional learning communities, students consistently outperform their peers (Lee & Smith, 1995, 1996; Lee, Smith, & Croninger, 1997; McLaughlin & Talbert, 2005). Virtually every study assessing the impact of professional development on student learning highlights the central importance of teachers struggling together to evaluate student work and discover ways to improve it (Elmore, Peterson, & McCarthey, 1996; Fullan, 1993; Hargreaves, 1994; Hawley & Valli, 2007; Miles & Darling-Hammond, 1998).

PRINCIPLES FOR INVESTING IN TEACHING QUALITY

Drawing on this research and our own work with schools, we identify four principles that high-performing schools follow to ensure consistent and always-improving quality of teaching. High-performing schools invest to continuously improve teaching quality by

A. Hiring and organizing staff to fit school needs in terms of expertise, philosophy, and schedule

B. Integrating significant resources for well-designed professional development that provides expert support to implement the school's core instructional design

C. Designing teacher work schedules to include blocks of collaborative planning time effectively used to improve classroom practice

D. Enacting systems that promote individual teacher growth through induction, leadership opportunities, professional development planning, evaluation, and compensation

Teaching Quality Design Principle A:
Hiring and Organizing Staff to Fit School
Needs in Terms of Expertise, Philosophy, and Schedule

In most schools, when a position comes open, it gets filled. A band teacher replaces a band teacher; a third-grade teacher replaces a third-grade teacher. At best, the principal and some teachers interview several candidates to informally assess fit and share information about the school. Strategic schools recognize that all else flows from successful hiring, and they employ hiring and assignment practices that link to a vision of what expertise, philosophy, and work schedule would best support the school's needs. Figure 3.1 contrasts the hiring process of typical and strategic schools.

Figure 3.1 Hiring and assignment practices of typical versus strategic schools

Practice	Typical School	Strategic School
Hiring plan begins with assessment of faculty and student priorities.	Positions posted as they become vacant.	Before posting a position, school leaders assess student need, staff capacity, and scheduling priorities to determine long-term staffing priorities and needs.
Job descriptions specify expertise, disposition, and work hours needed for each position.	Teacher job descriptions that apply generically to all teachers are used to describe position.	School leaders work ahead to define a clear set of desired traits, skills, and work schedules, keeping in mind the needs of the teacher's collaborative team, the school design, and the school's student population.
School actively works to ensure the quality of its hiring pool.	Schools interview candidates from standard hiring pool.	School actively encourages interns and finds opportunities for teachers needing part-time work.
Rigorous, multistep interview process allows school and candidate to assess fit.	Informal interview protocols assess fit and experience.	A well-designed protocol, combined with classroom lesson demonstrations, assesses candidate expertise, philosophy, and commitment.
Teacher assignments fit school and team needs.	Teacher teams are static; school leaders and assignment don't consider the mix of skills and experience.	School leaders carefully track whether new teachers are placed in supportive teams and make teaming changes as necessary to distribute expertise across grades and subjects.

The case vignettes presented in the following give more concrete examples of the types of things we see. Our point is not to advocate for any one of these school models, but to describe how their hiring process forms the foundation for strategic use of resources.

Central Park East High in New York City provides an example of how the school's instructional design shaped its school hiring strategy. In 1997, when we conducted the study, Central Park East had an extraordinary rate of college admittance of 90%, compared with a 50% rate in similar New York City schools. It accomplished this with no guidance counselors on staff to facilitate and support students with college readiness. Instead, Central Park East organized teachers and students into advisory groups, in which teachers performed the role traditionally associated with guidance counselors (Miles & Darling-Hammond, 1997). The school schedule also included significant collaborative time for teacher teams so that the teacher workday exceeded the contractually defined maximums. These design features (advisories to provide individual attention and extra teacher work time to enable teacher collaboration) complicated the Central Park hiring process. They required Central Park staff to maintain a certain philosophical orientation, to come equipped with an expanded set of skills and knowledge, and to be willing to work longer hours than teachers at neighboring schools for the same pay.

Central Park East's hiring process met these needs. School leaders recruited teachers who would relish playing a more active role in their student's lives and who were willing to work according to the adopted schedule. All new teachers signed a memorandum of understanding, in which they agreed to this role and the expanded hours. Signing the memorandum guaranteed the existing faculty that new teachers fully understood and accepted the school's instructional design. New teachers committed to implementing the school's critical strategies before they ever started working in the school.

The Mary Lyon Elementary School in Boston, Massachusetts, provides a more extreme example of design-specific hiring needs. At the time of the case study, the school fully integrated all students, including those with intensive special needs, into classrooms of 15 students with two teachers, a master and an intern. The school encouraged severely disabled students to attend so they could collect the resources and maintain low class sizes that allowed them to continue this somewhat radical mainstreaming. For this strategy to work, all Mary Lyon teachers needed to possess a passion for working with a range of student needs. They also had to have the certification to work with these children legally and the expertise needed to serve them well.

Principal Mary Nash understood that she could never organize a school with the expectation that all teachers could meet all needs of all students. So she didn't try. Instead, she and the leadership team approached the issue as a grade-level team challenge. They defined all the skills required for every grade-level team of teachers. This ideal combination of skills, which included working with gifted and limited English proficiency students, became the basis of the school's hiring process. All teachers needed a defined base of skills, but the needs of each position depended on the set of skills the existing teaching team possessed. Creating balanced, interdependent faculty teams and facilitating cooperation among team members became the vital work of the hiring process and the school's leadership team. In part by recruiting such a capable staff, this school quickly became one of the top-performing schools in Boston, a distinction it retains to this day.

The Graham and Parks, a school in Cambridge, Massachusetts, serving Grades 6 through 8, provides a third example of the ways in which various design features combine to influence the hiring strategy. Two middle-grade structures in particular had a seminal impact on who the school could hire:

- Middle-grade students were required to take a 100-minute humanities course each day that combined English with social studies.
- Subject-area teachers in each grade shared two common planning periods surrounding lunch to collaborate and engage in professional development.

These design elements influenced the philosophy, expertise, and working hours of the teachers needed. Graham and Parks school leaders needed to find teachers with an expertise in both of the two combined subjects who were committed to interdisciplinary instruction and to collaborating heavily with colleagues. They also needed to hire part-time elective teachers to cover for core teachers during the middle of the day because all of the teacher planning time occurred around the extended lunch period. Located in Cambridge, Massachusetts, a diverse urban city with a large concentration of students, artists, and writers, meant that finding part-time staff did not present an overwhelming challenge. The principal often marveled at the energy and creativity the part-time staff brought to student learning.

In each of the three examples just presented, the principals started the hiring process with a clear organizational and instructional strategy. This helped the school leaders outline the skills, attitudes, and work schedule they needed in their candidates. Having a clear instructional strategy and long-range hiring plan allows school leaders to define job descriptions specific to the school's needs. The job description could include the committees the new hire would be expected to participate in and specify the knowledge and skills required to meet other professional and team responsibilities.

Many of our case study schools go to extraordinary lengths to ensure they get the highest-quality candidates for job openings. Training student teachers helps to screen candidates and get a head start on inducting high-potential teachers. High Tech High School in San Diego, California, offers a new teacher training program that leads to full teacher credentials and ensures "first pick" of the best new teachers (Shields & Miles, 2008). Similarly, the Mary Lyon school in Boston referenced previously has also forged a partnership with a local university. Student teachers from the university receive a stipend for completing a yearlong internship with a master teacher at the Mary Lyon school (Miles & Darling-Hammond, 1997).

Teaching Quality Design Principle B: Integrating Significant Resources for Well-Designed Professional Development That Provides Expert Support to Implement the School's Core Instructional Design

Strategic schools are just as purposeful about how they build the capacity of the teachers already on staff as they are about hiring new teachers. Research shows that professional development can improve teacher practice and student performance (Carpenter, Fennema, Peterson, Chiang, & Loef, 1989; Cohen & Hill, 2000; Newmann & Associates, 1996; Stigler & Hiebert, 1999). But obviously, not all professional development activities are of equal value. High-performing schools improve student performance so successfully, in part, because they make sure to integrate resources for *well-designed* professional development that provides expert support for teachers to implement the school's core instructional design.

What Does It Mean to Design Professional Development Well?

A well-designed professional development plan combines the professional development activities and approaches most likely to improve student performance in a school's specific context. Strategic school leaders craft their own professional development plans because they know that student performance is most likely to improve when the professional development revolves around the specific curriculum and instructional materials that teachers use in their own classrooms (Cohen & Hill, 2000; Holland, 2005).

Researchers and reform support groups, including the National Staff Development Council and the National Partnership for Excellence and Accountability in Teaching, have identified a common set of characteristics of professional development factors likely to improve student performance (Hawley & Valli, 2007; Holland, 2005; Knapp, McCaffrey, & Swanson, 2003). To summarize, the type of professional development most likely to improve student performance

1. Evolves out of the analysis of student performance

2. Is organized as school-based, collaborative problem solving

3. Focuses on the implementation of specific content-based curriculum and instructional practices

4. Is scheduled as part of the everyday work of teaching

5. Includes follow-up and coaching

6. Promotes coherent, schoolwide design

7. Promotes accountability for improved practice and student performance

As with any list of design principles, well-meaning school leaders or professional development providers can design offerings that appear to meet these criteria, but that actually do not reflect the nuances identified in the research or the intended meaning of the carefully chosen words. Many professional development activities may appear to meet these criteria or to embrace these design principles in name while not meeting them in reality. To help clarify how school planning teams can successfully apply these design principles, Figure 3.2 contrasts the ways typical schools and high-performing schools might implement them.

Figure 3.2 suggests that continuously improving schools and teachers view professional development as a way of life. In these schools, every lesson represents an opportunity to learn something new about how to help students further their understanding. Teachers in these schools use common planning time to work on lesson plans together, dig through assessment data and discover what worked and what didn't, and discuss how to help individual students. In such high-performing schools, teachers may not even describe this collective work and reflection as "professional development." Instead, it is simply part of the teaching enterprise.

Four Professional Development Designs
That Improve Student Performance

A number of prominent professional development designs meet these more stringent criteria and illustrate the critical characteristics of

Figure 3.2   How typical and strategic schools implement well-designed
professional development

What the Research Says About Well-Designed Professional Development	How Typical Schools Design Professional Development	How Strategic Schools Design Professional Development
Evolves out of analysis of student performance	• Teachers learn how to analyze student performance data. • Teachers receive professional development in topic areas where student performance is poor.	• School leaders and teacher teams use student performance data to determine areas of focus and set school improvement goals. • Using data on their own student's performance on tests and classroom assignments, teachers identify instructional areas for improvement and monitor their effectiveness.
Organized as school-based, collaborative problem solving	• Groups of teachers from any school participate. • Professional development takes place in a school or classroom.	• Teams of teachers in the same school whose members share subjects or students collaborate around assessment and instruction.
Focused on implementation of specific, content-based curriculum and instructional practices	• Instructional methods taught separately from content or specific curriculum materials.	• Professional development happens in the context of the specific curriculum and instructional materials the teachers are using.
Scheduled as part of the everyday work of teaching	• Teachers have the same 45-minute period free from instruction as some other teachers do. • Schoolwide staff development happens about four times a year on staff development days.	• Time is structured to allow sufficient, regular time for the right groups to collaborate.

What the Research Says About Well-Designed Professional Development	How Typical Schools Design Professional Development	How Strategic Schools Design Professional Development
Includes follow-up and coaching	• Teachers have periodic access to coaches or mentors often not connected to their daily work.	• Teachers practice new strategies and review impact with expert support throughout their careers.
Promotes a coherent, schoolwide design	• Periodic, scattered introduction of new concepts, frameworks, and tools with no adjustment to match school or individual teacher needs.	• Content is consistent with the language, instructional methods, priorities, and timing of the school's instructional design.
Promotes accountability	• There is no measurement or discussion of changed instructional practice or student performance results.	• Improved instruction and student performance are expected, measured, and reflected on. Teacher evaluations require improved instruction.

well-designed professional development. Their use has resulted in demonstrable improvement in student performance. We present four such models here as case examples:

1. The Collaborative Coaching Laboratories (CCL) model implemented in New York City and Boston Public Schools (Boston Plan for Excellence, 2003)

2. The Lesson Study model (Stigler & Hiebert, 1999)

3. Education Trust's Standards in Practice model (Supovitz & Corcoran, 2000)

4. The America's Choice comprehensive school design model in schools across the country (Bodilly, 1998; May, Supovitz, & Perda, 2004)

1. Collaborative Coaching Laboratories. In the CCL model, a team of teachers works with a coach who will support them intensely during one or more six- to eight-week cycles, throughout the year. Each team

- chooses a topic for inquiry (often with support from school leaders);
- reads and discusses the topic, learning together;
- observes each other teaching (may begin with a coach demonstration);
- debriefs using a protocol that focuses on teacher practice and deemphasizes individual competence;
- works with a coach in individual sessions, with the coach observing, demonstrating, and providing feedback to each team member; and
- meets less formally between intense cycles.

Boston Public Schools implemented the CCL model across all schools in the district. Well implemented, the CCL model clearly meets the most stringent definitions of effective professional development:

- Teachers, school leaders, and instructional coaches choose the area of focus together based on student performance and teacher needs.
- Collaborative teacher teams receive expert coaching as they improve their practice together over a period of time.
- Teachers learn in their own classrooms as they try new methods, observe each other, and reflect on success or failure.
- Accountability is fostered by peer and coach observations and follow-up sessions.
- Especially effective leadership teams deliberately link the effect of the collaborative coaching work to student performance and ensure that coaching focuses on the lower-performing students and teachers. (For more information on the CCL model, see www.bpe.org.)

2. The Lesson Study Model. Stigler and Hiebert (1999) developed Lesson Study by observing teams of teachers in Japan. In Lesson Study, groups of four to six teachers meet together for a two- to four-week period to thoroughly plan every detail of a lesson together. Then, they teach the planned lesson (sometimes observing each other). Afterward, they meet again to revise the lessons based on what they learned using the lesson the first time. Typically, the tested lessons are then made public for other teachers to use. Lesson study groups can be an ongoing part of the work of teacher teams, a grade-level team for example, or they can exist only for the life of a single lesson study. (For more information on the Lesson Study model, see www.tc.columbia.edu/lessonstudy.)

3. Standards in Practice. Cincinnati Public Schools adopted Standards in Practice across its elementary schools in 1999. Student performance increased in schools where teacher teams implemented the practices with fidelity (Supovitz & Corcoran, 2000). Education Trust's Standards in

Practice model groups teachers who are teaching a common grade or subject or who share the same students. The model is designed to help make sure teachers

- give assignments that align with specific student standards,
- can determine whether the student met the standard being addressed, and
- know how to adjust instruction in response to assessed performance.

To accomplish these objectives, teachers work initially with an experienced facilitator who uses a protocol to help them learn to dissect assignments, match up learning goals, and review student work and other assessments. (See www2.edtrust.org.)

4. America's Choice. America's Choice is an example of a Comprehensive School Reform Design Model (sometimes called the CSRD model). Comprehensive reform models like America's Choice or Success for All are based on the philosophy that a successful instructional approach requires a comprehensive integration of curriculum, assessment, teacher skills, and instructional strategies. Their comprehensive approach attempts to align all of a school's instructional and support strategies by moving them to one provider in one comprehensive program. America's Choice's research-based professional development also includes an explicit program to introduce new material and to support principals and teachers over time. By integrating professional development so tightly and sequencing it to meet needs as they arise, professional development becomes highly relevant and rewarding for teachers and principals. (See www.americaschoice.org.)

Research supports the approach taken by America's Choice. For instance, a majority of Rochester, New York, Public Schools adopted the America's Choice model in 2001. Research by an outside evaluator subsequently showed significant improvement in student performance in the America's Choice schools above that seen by other district schools (Bodilly, 1998; May et al., 2004).

Each of these four models can be implemented in ways that meet the most stringent criteria for well-designed professional development, but faithful implementation is not easy and requires strategic school leaders to consider the other principles of professional development: hiring strategically, creating effective collaboration time, and supporting the individual career growth of each teacher. It also requires them to ensure the right type and amount of expert support. We turn now to this topic.

How Do Strategic Schools Think About Expert Support?

What is the role of the expert in improving instruction? How much is enough? What is the right type of support? Should we hire experts from inside the school or outside it? In many schools

- Teachers work independently, autonomous in their own classrooms.
- Feedback is infrequent, little more than an occasional observation.
- Mentors meet with new teachers infrequently to share tips or help them adjust.
- All non-novice teachers are given indistinguishable roles.
- All teachers are paid on the same scale, which doesn't reward better instruction.
- Any teacher leadership opportunities (e.g., department head) focus on administration. In high schools, department heads sometimes play a leadership role in sharing expertise, but often this job tends toward administration rather than knowledge sharing (McLaughlin & Talbert, 2003, 2005).
- Expert support comes mostly from workshops or college courses.

By contrast, high-performing schools actively manage expert support because they view teaching as a collective effort to ensure student learning across grades and subjects. They know that this challenge is hard enough to require joint effort and multiple kinds of expertise. High-performing schools strategically leverage experts both on staff and from outside to improve their teaching practice. Where they need outside assistance, they reach out to introduce new knowledge and skills and build needed school capacity.

Are Coaches the Answer?

We are often asked whether we recommend that a school hire instructional coaches. It is a complicated question. In schools in which teacher capacity or student performance results are low, the use of coaches has become increasingly widespread (Neufeld & Roper, 2003). An Education Trust (1999) study of high-poverty schools that had dramatically improved student performance found that each of these schools employed expert help to improve their instructional practice. The increase of coaches is fueled by district leaders who assign coaches to low-performing schools and by comprehensive school reform models like America's Choice and Success for All, which require schools to purchase expert coaching, because it is a centerpiece of their models. States, too, are mandating coaching for low-performing schools.

The results of assigning coaches have been mixed. This suggests that simplistic adoption will not lead to success (Neufeld & Roper, 2003). An effective coaching strategy requires school leaders to clearly specify the goals and purposes of the coaching model, to map out the concrete activities and practices the coaches will be required to engage in or support, and to create a detailed implementation plan.

What is the purpose of coaching? Why would a school choose or not choose it as an improvement strategy? The term *coach*, now used so often in education settings, has lost its immediate reference to sports. In sports, a coach who has more experience and expertise than his or her players is responsible to work with and inspire them to improve their skills, their execution of strategy, and their teamwork.

What is the method of coaching? How does the coach succeed or fail? The sports coach

- designs and leads practices that address individual and team needs,
- provides advice and support during games (implementation),
- dissects game videos (performance) individually and with the team, and
- uses new knowledge to improve weaknesses and build on strengths in practice.

Come the next game, coaches expect team and individual play—and the game results—to improve based on their work. Coaches can bench players who do not perform well. If the team fails persistently, the coach can be fired, too.

In sports, coaches choose this role as their career. These coaches work to develop their skills as coaches. They need to and have the opportunity to acquire specialized skills that go beyond the game. In more complicated sports, such as baseball, the coaching roles become more specialized. Specialist coaches work with subsets of the team on discrete skills and roles, such as pitching, hitting, and running bases.

The coaching model assumes that players improve by exposing their practice to constructive criticism and by practicing together over time. There is a mutual sense of accountability. Coaches and players feel accountable to one another. Management holds them directly responsible for performing well and improving over time.

Although the purpose of a coach in sports is very similar to that of an instructional coach in a school (improving performance through feedback), there are places where the analogy falls apart that help to explain why some schools succeed with coaches whereas others flounder. Three primary reasons include

1. **Underspecified roles and skills for coaches.** When roles for coaches are unclear, schools may mistakenly hire a teacher who is experienced, charismatic, or highly regarded to be a coach even though the teacher may lack other skills necessary for good coaching, such as the ability to facilitate group work, assess student or teacher needs, or provide criticism to adults in nonthreatening ways. This role can change over time and with needed changes to the coaching model.

2. **Unclear models for how, when, and why coaches work with teachers.** When the model is unspecified, schools can go to the expense of hiring a coach without setting up time for the coach to work with teachers and teacher teams or without truly understanding whether they need sophisticated subject expertise or a stronger focus on collaborative methods. The faculty's experience with collaboration and overall teacher capacity will thus determine the model chosen. The model chosen will, in turn, impact the skill set needed by the coach.

3. **How coaches and teachers are held accountable.** Instructional coaches are not in a position where they can "bench" teachers or fire them. Practically speaking, this means that mutual accountability needs to come from norms or from other structures that exist in the school. In many cases, norms do not support teacher accountability and continuous improvement of instructional practices.

In short, the existence of a coaching strategy is not sufficient to ensure the effectiveness of expert support. Success requires clear goals and expectations for the role and skills of the coach, specified times and ways for the coaches to interact with teachers, and structures and attitudes that foster mutual accountability for continuous improvement. The case of Perspectives Charter School in Chicago will provide a concrete example of how one school provided its own expert support.

Strategic School Case Example

Perspectives Charter School, in the district of Chicago, provides a powerful example of using internal experts to build capacity. A small school of 300 students, Perspectives employed four part-time instructional leaders who each coached, mentored, and evaluated four to eight teachers in one subject. Two of these teachers also taught for half of the school day. Instructional leaders served as the content coaches for the school. To fulfill their responsibilities, the instructional leaders

- conducted formal evaluations of teachers twice each year;
- observed teachers weekly, including preobservation and postobservation sessions to plan and debrief the lesson with each teacher;
- met teachers individually to review their 60-day goals;
- facilitated common planning sessions for content and grade-level teams;
- planned and facilitated professional development in summer and throughout the year; and
- met with the dean of academics twice monthly to refine professional development plans and generate topics based on classroom observations.

Perspectives' instructional leaders also received professional development themselves to help them reflect on and improve their own practice as coaches. For example, they received training in how to conduct three- to five-minute observations focused on curriculum, instruction, and classroom environment. The principal selected instructional leaders based on her observation of their ability to improve student achievement, motivate students, adhere to the "Perspectives Way," and promote satisfied parents (Shields & Miles, 2008).

Although the instructional leadership model worked well for Perspectives, it is clear that hiring a coach or identifying an expert support advisor is not sufficient by itself to meet the needs of schools. In the next section, we discuss how schools set up collaborative teams and generate time in the day for them to work with each other. This has an enormous impact on whether expert support can be delivered in an effective manner.

Teaching Quality Design Principle C: Designing Teacher Work Schedules to Include Blocks of Collaborative Planning Time Effectively Used to Improve Classroom Practice

Research on school improvement highlights the need for significant collaborative planning time for teachers. It notes that the lack of such time creates a critical barrier to reform (Neufeld & Roper, 2003; Raywid, 1993; Swaim & Swaim, 1999). The length of time for collaboration is also critical. One study found that teachers need at least three hours each week to work together to improve instruction (Bodilly, 1998). Finally, another study that analyzed student performance data over time found that common planning time, along with teacher control over instructional decisions, were the two most important workplace predictors of student performance (Rowan, Chiang, & Miller, 1997).

Using collaboration time wisely is essential because creating it costs so much. As Figure 3.3 shows, teacher time can comprise up to 65% of a school's total professional development investment (when we include the cost of collaborative planning time).

Unfortunately, most schools provide little to no time for teacher collaboration. Again, the reasons for this are largely historical. Schools evolved in a time and in ways such that collaboration among teachers was not emphasized. Teacher autonomy became the norm instead, to the point that many teachers resist giving up independent time even when contracts allow this time to be dedicated for collaboration (Goodlad, 1984). Rigid bell schedules reinforced this value system by isolating teachers in classrooms and allowing them only infrequent interaction with their peers and by chopping time into blocks too short (45 to 55 minutes typically) to be used effectively. Many teacher contracts *require* instruction-free periods to be spread over the day. Other problems include a general lack of capacity and accountability, as evidenced by

- vague (unspecified) expectations for how administrators think common time should be used, which can confuse or frustrate teacher teams that attempt collaboration;
- lack of knowledge by faculty and administration on how to work together effectively, which can result in administrators talking *at* teachers instead of working *with* them; and
- unclear responsibilities for individual teachers within groups, which can result in dropped assignments or a generally ineffective use of time.

Figure 3.3   Chicago Public Schools: Components of school professional development expenditures

Type of Expenditure	Percentage of School Professional Development Spending, Not Including Common Planning Time	Percentage of School Professional Development Spending, Including Common Planning Time
Training and coaching	57%	28%
Teacher time	31%	65%
Tuition and fees	5%	3%
Travel and transportation	4%	2%
Materials and supplies	3%	2%

Strategic schools, on the other hand, provide significantly greater time for teachers to collaborate and have found ways to structure it in longer blocks (Miles & Darling-Hammond, 1998). Leaders specify clear expectations and standards and provide rubrics and protocols as tools to support the specified use. Expert support is made available, especially for teams that may not have experience collaborating. Time is used to review formative assessments or other student work to ensure that assignments align to standards and that students are meeting them. Collaborative time is a time for teachers to plan lessons jointly, to receive expert support in content areas, to model effective instructional practices, to reflect together on instructional practice, and to receive feedback from peers or from subject experts.

The differences between typical schools and strategic schools are summarized in Figure 3.4.

In Chapter 8, we will share specific examples of and strategies for developing a schedule and plan for creating effective collaborative time for teachers. Although much of the professional development at the school level aims at teacher teams and takes place through collaboration, teachers have their own individual growth needs as well. We turn now to explore this important component of a professional development strategy.

Teaching Quality Design Principle D: Enacting Systems That Promote Individual Teacher Growth Through Induction, Leadership Opportunities, Professional Development Planning, Evaluation, and Compensation

Although teachers grow professionally together, they also have individual professional development needs over their careers. These needs depend on their career stage as well as their personal interests and skills. Figure 3.5 shows one way of defining the stages of a teaching career. All new teachers begin as novices in the classroom, and they move at various rates toward proficiency depending on their prior experiences, skills in different areas, and commitment. Research shows that experience improves the impact of teaching, but only through the first three to five years (Murnane, 1991; Rice, 2002b). After this, practice improves only through the combination of commitment, individual strengths, and continued opportunity (Ingersoll, 1999). Since professional development needs vary in time and nature, it can be difficult to devise a school-level strategy for supporting them. For this reason, districts often play a major role in providing support for individual teacher growth. Districts can collect enough teachers together who have similar support and training needs.

Figure 3.4   Collaboration time in a typical versus strategic school

Planning Time Characteristic	Typical School	Strategic School
Amount of time	Little to no time for teacher collaboration is built into school day; teachers may talk during lunch or after school; individual planning time may or may not be scheduled so teacher teams share planning period.	Weekly collaborative planning sessions are embedded in the bell schedule; collaborative time is provided in addition to individual time; schedule may provide daily extended sessions.
Length of sessions	Time, when provided at all, is organized into one-period blocks of 45 to 60 minutes.	Extended sessions of 90 minutes or more are incorporated regularly; professional development days are spread over the year.
Expectations for use of time	No clarity around individual roles or group tasks; no written standards or rubrics; teachers may be told what to do or given specific tasks by departmental administrators.	Expectations are clearly and frequently communicated by word and in writing; research-supported rubrics and protocols are provided for use during collaboration time.
How time is used	Teacher teams meet only infrequently and decide how to use collective time; some sessions may be usurped by departmental training, announcements, or other activities.	Teacher teams review assessments/student work, receive content support, plan lessons, reflect together on instructional practice, model effective instruction, and receive feedback from peers or subject experts.
Availability of expert support	Principal or other centrally housed expert may visit team on occasion on centrally defined initiatives.	Expert support is provided to all teams with emphasis on teams that may lack internal capacity or when expectations around collaboration are new.

The idiosyncratic nature of teacher training needs also contributes to the traditional approach, which leaves individual professional development up to the teacher's discretion. Teacher contracts often require districts to set aside dollars for teachers to take coursework of their own choosing.

Figure 3.5   Stages of a teaching career

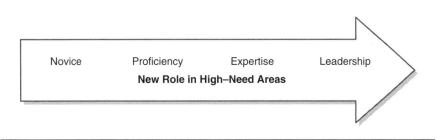

Yet research shows that the most effective professional development takes place in the context of the specific classroom and around the challenges the individual teacher faces in improving student performance (Hawley & Valli, 2007; Knapp et al., 2003). Furthermore, high-functioning professional communities rely on *all* teachers reaching proficiency and a large portion of teachers playing leadership roles such as mentoring, coaching, practicing team leadership, or doing teacher evaluation. These leadership roles require teachers to develop new skills that involve working with adults to encourage changed behavior, creating teams, and managing organizations effectively. Because schools benefit when teachers develop these skills and they can develop them best in the school and classroom context, strategic school leaders purposefully work to promote each individual.

Besides supporting the career stages just described, schools might also need to be concerned with providing remediation and "retraining." By remediation, we mean support needed by an underperforming teacher at any point of the teacher's career. "Retraining" refers to situations in which a school's instructional design might demand that an individual teacher or group of teachers acquires new skills or certification status. For example, a school might determine that all teachers should acquire dual certification in special education and so develop a schoolwide approach to providing professional development on site to make it easier for teachers to do this. Or the school might plan to implement a new humanities curriculum that combines English and social studies, requiring that teachers be certified and competent in the subject matter for both subjects.

Figure 3.6 contrasts the kind of individual teacher professional development that happens in typical schools with that of strategic schools.

Leaders of high-performing schools recognize that teachers need ongoing opportunities and support as they move through different stages of their careers. They systematically groom teachers for leadership roles by creating individual plans for each teacher, evaluating them regularly, organizing

Figure 3.6   Professional development system in a typical versus strategic school

Components of Individual Professional Development Systems	Typical School	Strategic School
Induction support	• Short orientation • Mentor assigned by school or district to provide for periodic consultation	• Research-based designs that provide deep, ongoing support • Integrates the district-provided support with its own school needs • Assigns new teachers manageable challenges
Leadership development	• Based on individual teacher initiative	• Systematic provision of growth opportunities linked to school needs
Individual professional development plans	• Small financial support for individual coursework or conference participation at teacher initiation • Limited use of individual growth plans	• Regular review of professional development plans that inform opportunities
Evaluation	• Infrequent and compliance oriented • Not linked to professional development	• Regular evaluations that link to professional development, support, and opportunities provided
Compensation	• Linked to years of experience and coursework taken	• Works within system to reward teachers who demonstrate expertise

teacher teams, delegating responsibility, and sharing leadership opportunities. Although school districts often organize mentoring programs, strategic school leaders know that district programs for new teachers vary both in quality and intensity (Ingersoll & Smith, 2004). They find ways to supplement or redirect district support when needed to better align with school needs and ensure sufficient, appropriate support (Johnson, 2007).

A review of research (Ingersoll, 1999; Johnson, 2007; Moir, 2003) suggests that effective induction programs

- allow meaningful interaction, classroom support, and observation;
- provide sufficient time for individual teacher planning and collaboration;
- include curriculum guidance and materials if possible;
- match professional development to the new teacher's individual needs;
- include frequent opportunities for reflection, assessment, and evaluation; and
- avoid giving new teachers unreasonable numbers of students to teach (teacher load), the most challenging sets of student needs, or too many distinct courses to "prep" for (teacher preps).

Thus far, we have discussed mentoring as way for schools to help new teachers grow in their careers. Mentoring is also an example of how to help experienced teachers develop leadership skills. Being a mentor of a new teacher does require that teachers develop new skills.

In addition to being effective teachers, mentors also need to understand and be able to explain what makes their teaching effective. They must be able to pinpoint ways for new teachers to build their skills (Moir, 2003). Mentoring is but one of many leadership opportunities that school leaders can offer teachers who wish to share their expertise and develop their leadership capacity. Other positions include coach, team leader, curriculum chair, assessment coordinator, and similar roles. School leaders who create individual development plans for teachers can deliberately and systematically nurture the leadership capacity of their schools.

The high-performing New York City District 2 provides an example of how creating individual professional development plans for all teachers can increase the overall level of teacher leadership and improve student performance. In this district, each teacher was required to create a narrative version of his or her individual goals and objectives for each year. The teachers' personal goals and objectives had to be explicitly linked to the school's overall goals. Teachers described how they would implement their goals and how they would measure whether the goals had been accomplished. As teachers filled out their goals and objectives form, they were asked to reflect on how their goals and objectives would be aided by collaboration with their colleagues. The completed forms did not hide under a paperweight on the principal's desk. The individual plans of teachers fed into the principal's schoolwide professional development plan. All of the plans helped the superintendent and his staff allocate time and resources (Elmore & Burney, 1999).

By linking individual planning to school goals and to individual and collective professional development support, schools begin to create a cycle of ongoing improvement. Evaluation and assessment of performance play a key role in this virtuous cycle. Figure 3.7 shows these links and how they reinforce each other.

As teachers and their leaders jointly assess and evaluate what they need to learn, they inform the individual teacher professional development plan as well as the school improvement plan. This assessment helps school leaders understand how to structure teams, assign responsibilities, and grow teacher skills that are useful to the teacher and the school. As each cycle raises teacher performance, the entire school attains a higher level of proficiency. Students learn more. The school moves on to address new challenges.

The National Institute for Excellence in Teaching (NIET) provides a concrete example of how strategically minded school leaders can organize to grow the skills of individual teachers and the school through its Teacher Advancement Program (TAP). School districts across the country have begun to implement TAP with such positive results that the U.S. Department of Education recently awarded $34 million to extend it across more districts (Keller, 2006). Figure 3.8 displays the roles, work assignments, and stipends of master teachers and mentors (NIET, 2005).

A TAP elementary school of 500 would assign two full-time master teachers to oversee the work of teams of teachers, provide demonstrations, and evaluate teacher performance. They might also assign four classroom teachers to serve as mentors. (The exact number of mentors

Figure 3.7   Organic cycle of teacher support and evaluation

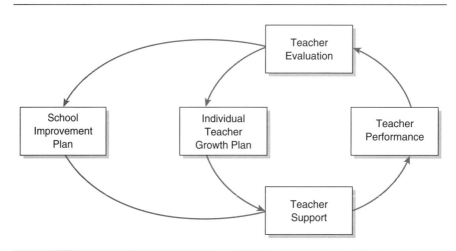

Figure 3.8   Elements of the Teacher Advancement Program

Master Teachers	*Two Full-Time, Out-of-the-Classroom Teachers*
Role	Oversee work of cluster groups; team teach with colleagues and provide demonstrations; facilitate curriculum and assessment planning; observe and evaluate teachers four to six times/year
Stipend	Average of $7,500 per teacher
Extra work days	Average of 10 extra days/year
Mentor Teachers	*Four Classroom Teachers*
Role	Plan and facilitate cluster group meetings; team teach with colleagues and provide demonstrations; observe and evaluate teachers four to six times/year
Stipend	Average of $3,500 per teacher
Extra work days	Average of seven extra days/year
Release time	Five hours/week to meet with cluster groups
Performance bonuses	All teachers are eligible for bonuses based on value-added model of student improvement in classrooms and schoolwide

depends on the number of new teachers the school has.) Mentors do not have formal evaluation responsibility, as they aim to create a safe place for experimentation and failure. Mentors have five hours of release time each week to work with new teachers. The TAP model also rewards teacher proficiency by providing bonuses to teachers who improve their performance. Performance bonuses aim to tighten the links between the parts of the cycle of teacher improvement described previously (NIET, 2005).

Consider also how the Academy of the Pacific Rim (APR) fosters the career growth of teachers in the school's context. APR is a charter school serving Grades 6 through 12 in Hyde Park, Massachusetts. During the school year, APR devotes two hours of each week on Wednesday afternoons to professional development. During this time, the school meets as a whole, by departments, or by grade-level teams.

APR provides all of its teachers with a number of opportunities to develop professionally:

- newly hired teachers are invited to work with colleagues in their department for the last few weeks of the APR school year (receiving a stipend);

- new teachers are assigned a mentor (with both receiving a stipend);
- new teachers meet formally with the principal once a week for an hour;
- newly hired teachers meet together once a month, with an experienced teacher; and finally
- each APR teacher is allotted $300 for individual professional development.

These activities, in addition to the schoolwide professional development work, the commitment to creating a powerful and coherent school culture, and the provision of individual attention to students, are strategically linked to compensation through an innovative bonus system (see Figure 3.9).

In this way, the APR makes a strong statement to its faculty that the goal of school is to raise student achievement. As Figure 3.9 reveals, 50% of the bonus is based on schoolwide performance measures and is either dispersed to all staff members or to none (Shields & Miles, 2008).

Figure 3.9   Building the bonus at the Academy of the Pacific Rim

Factor	Percentage of Bonus
Individual Administrative Review (50%)	
Teaching	15%
Professionalism	10%
Individual goals	10%
Reinforcing school culture	5%
Advising	5%
Collaboration	5%
Team Achievement Bonus (50%)	
Parent/guardian survey	5%
Massachusetts Comprehensive Assessment System (MCAS) passing rate	25%
MCAS proficiency and improvement	20%

SOURCE: Shields, Regis and Miles, Karen, 2008. Strategic Designs. "Building the Bonus at the Academy of the Pacific Rim." Reprinted with permission.

Teacher compensation and evaluation systems *should* support and reward teachers for improving their proficiency over their career, but most schools can't do that. They operate in districts that raise teacher salaries based on years of service and course credits. Strategic principals find other ways to reward their best teachers. They find resources for stipends to compensate teachers who take on leadership roles. They schedule an extra free period for the most-expert teachers so these teachers can coach their peers. They reimburse teachers who attend professional conferences or participate in networks across schools.

Strategic school leaders are creating a new paradigm for building teacher capacity. Instead of viewing teaching quality as something that is best developed individually as teachers enroll in off-site courses, these school leaders see increasing the quality of instruction as the central focus of in-school activities. They actively create opportunities for teachers and teams of teachers to grow skills, knowledge, and networks that meet the goals of each teacher and the school community. To succeed, strategic school leaders have to challenge practices, assumptions, and norms that are continuously reinforced by dysfunctional salary structures and other district practices. These structures, built to support the old goals and methods of schooling, invest scarce dollars to support teachers taking outside courses or attending district-provided professional development that may not fit school or teacher needs. Strategic leaders succeed because they create a vision of how they will build the collective and individual knowledge and skills they need. And then they act on it.

Creating Individual 4
Attention and
Personal Learning
Environments

Anyone involved with schools intuitively understands the importance of individual attention. Parents and teachers fight for small class sizes, and legislators require them. Individualized education plans for special-education students require individual aides and small-group instruction. As we will describe in the following, research has attempted to quantify the impact of class size and small-group instruction at the elementary school level. A growing body of research on how people learn and the power of relationships further clarifies the kinds of attention that promise to promote learning.

For instance, leading scholars on brain research insist that early, intensive learning experiences actually change the structure of the brain and facilitate learning later in life (Bransford, Brown, & Cocking, 1999). They suggest that some parts of the brain may be ready to learn earlier than others and that "different kinds of learning goals require different approaches to instruction" (Bransford et al., 1999). This implies that effective instruction must be connected with the experience and knowledge (both accurate and inaccurate) of the learner. Bransford and colleagues (1999) argued that ongoing feedback to learners, as opposed to feedback given at the end of a unit or term, is essential because it helps learners adjust their understanding and effort.

PRINCIPLES FOR PROVIDING INDIVIDUAL ATTENTION

The high-performing schools we studied create individual attention and personal learning environments for all students by

E. Assessing student learning to adjust instruction and support

F. Creating smaller group sizes and reducing teacher loads in high-need areas

G. Organizing structures that foster personal relationships between students and teachers

Although these schools could have chosen to provide equal amounts of individual attention for all subjects, for all students, for all relationships, for all purposes, they didn't. Instead, they strategically realigned resources to target individual attention where it made the most sense.

Individual Attention Principle E: Assessing Student Learning to Adjust Instruction and Support

To provide individual attention to students, teachers must have an in-depth understanding of each student's mastery of skills and what the student needs to reach his or her potential. Ongoing assessment of student learning provides teachers with immediate and relevant data that can be used to build individual plans for success and support students in ways that will make the most impact on their own learning.

Teachers gather a variety of information about their students: They conduct exams and quizzes, grade homework and writing assignments, ask questions, listen to class discussions, and observe student interactions. These activities are all "formative assessments" of student work—*formative*, because they are used to determine what students are learning along the way and to adjust teaching accordingly. They also give teachers the opportunity to rethink lesson plans or homework, regroup students flexibly throughout the day, and provide tutoring or extend learning time for students who struggle. Formative assessments also benefit students by providing an immediate opportunity to see where they need to focus their efforts.

These advantages are echoed in research findings that consistently demonstrate that formative assessments have a profound, positive impact on achievement. Black and Wiliam (1998) summarized their extensive review of decades of research on the power of assessment as follows:

> The research reported here shows conclusively that formative assessment does improve student learning. The gains in achievement appear to be quite considerable, and as noted earlier; amongst the largest ever reported for educational interventions . . . equivalent to raising the mathematics achievement score of an "average"

country like England, New Zealand or the United States into the "top five" after the Pacific Rim countries of Singapore, Korea, Japan and Hong Kong. (p. 71)

Note the distinction between formative assessments and summative assessments. Some schools believe they are doing well with assessment because they conduct several rounds of summative or benchmark assessments annually. However, these important assessments differ in purpose from formative assessments. They are designed to determine what has been learned over the course of a unit, a grade, or a career (summative assessments), or to compare schools and students with each other or against standards (benchmark assessments). Because they are given infrequently or at the end of the year, such tests do not typically provide information on student progress in a timely way. They cannot take the place of a rigorous system of formal and informal formative assessments that allow teachers to tailor their lessons to individual needs along the way.

Strategic schools use ongoing assessments as a way not only to better support student learning, but to improve teacher practice. Figure 4.1 compares the assessment systems of a typical school with that of a strategic school.

In virtually every high-performing school design we have studied, including all of the comprehensive school reform models being spread nationwide, instruction and teacher collaboration revolve around using formative assessment data. For instance, the widely implemented Success for All model structures 90 minutes of daily reading instruction in all elementary grades. (For more information, see www.successforall.org.) Teachers in these schools use formative assessments at six-week intervals throughout the year to build both homogeneous and heterogeneous reading groups that support students in tackling different literacy skills. Similarly, the America's Choice model provides formative assessment tools that support the literacy and math curriculum as well as professional development to support school leaders and teachers in using these formative assessments to adjust instruction. (For more information on America's Choice, see www.americaschoice.org.) These ongoing assessments give teachers a deep understanding of each student's progress and enable them to group and support students depending on their mastery of the skills.

At the secondary level, Tech Boston Academy, a high school that prepares students for careers in technology, computers, and engineering, uses formative assessments to track and review individual student progress.

Figure 4.1   Assessing learning and adjusting instruction in typical versus strategic schools

Practice	Typical School	Strategic School
Teachers assess students on an ongoing basis.	Schools conduct rounds of summative or benchmark assessments to determine what was learned over a unit, course, or year.	Schools conduct formative assessments throughout the year to ensure teachers know whether students are learning what they should be as the year progresses—not only after the year or unit is over.
Teachers use assessment results to improve practice.	Teachers acquire much information about student progress through homework or quizzes, daily interactions, and standardized assessment results. However, many teachers in typical schools do *not* regularly use these data to adjust instruction and create personal learning environments.	Teachers examine results from ongoing assessments and use these data to improve lessons and tailor instruction to meet specific student needs.
Teachers use common time to examine assessment data and determine next steps based on findings.	Teachers examine assessment data alone, without consulting peers.	Schools provide blocks of common planning time during which teachers may collaborate with their colleagues to interpret and then use the data to improve schoolwide practice.
Teachers use a common approach to evaluation.	Teachers develop their own assessments classroom by classroom or use curriculum-issued tests as they complete specific units.	Teachers align their evaluation strategies across the schools. For example, all elementary schools might perform reading assessments every six weeks and compare progress. A secondary school might use a schoolwide writing prompt to examine writing skills. Teachers are then able to use this common strategy to discuss findings and adjust instruction accordingly.

Focusing on prevention before remediation, the headmaster and the student support coordinator examine all entering students' records for test data, attendance, and behavior patterns. In addition, the school administers benchmark assessments in September and other formative assessments throughout the year, tracking student progress over time. Importantly, the teachers then meet to discuss the data—at the beginning of the year they meet for up to three hours a week—and identify students who are struggling or need a more challenging class placement. Findings are shared with administrators and student support providers, and action plans are developed for each individual student. Students spend about 45 minutes a day in a "Project Room" period, where they receive customized individual support assigned by their teacher teams. In some cases, if groups of students share common needs such as test-taking strategies, they might use this period for a short-lived course on this subject (Shields & Miles, 2008).

Individual Attention Principle F: Creating Smaller Group Sizes and Reducing Teacher Loads in High-Need Areas

The effect of class sizes on student performance is by far the most popular and researched strategy for increasing individual attention. Although parents and teachers routinely focus on reducing class size as a way to improve student performance, the research tells us that reducing class sizes for all students in all subjects does not guarantee improved student achievement (Hanushek, 1997; Mosteller, 1995).

However, a growing number of studies show that strategic reductions in class size can make important—but not necessarily large—differences. The widely cited Student Teacher Achievement Ratio (STAR) study, which reduced class sizes randomly for some students and not others, showed that class-size reduction in the early grades (PreK through second grade) can make a measurable and lasting difference in student achievement, especially for students from low-income families (Word, Johnson, & Bain, 1990). However, small reductions in class size make little difference in student performance. Achievement increases predictably only when class sizes are reduced to 13 to 17 students—or lower. The STAR study estimates that student achievement in both math and English increased by four percentile points in the first year and one percentile point in the next two years when class sizes in the early grades dropped 30% from 22 to 15. Other research suggests that if teachers don't change their classroom practice to take advantage of class-size reductions, there is no reason to expect improved student achievement (Finn, Gerber, Achilles, & Boyd-Zaharias, 2001; Mishel & Rothstein, 2002; Mosteller, 1995; Zurawski, 2003).

This research has motivated some 40 states to mandate class sizes of no more than 20 for primary-grade (K–3) students (EdWeek, 2007).

Reducing class sizes requires significant resources. A 32% drop in class sizes from 22 to 15 as cited previously would cost one third of the average teacher compensation, an increase in spending of about 20% or more than $1,000 per pupil for a small increase in student achievement. This strategy needs to be compared with other ways of investing to improve student performance. In schools we have worked with, we have identified four major categories of strategies for increasing individual attention in content areas. These include

- Class-size reduction
- Small-group instruction in specific subject areas
- Individual tutoring
- Reducing teacher load in secondary schools

Allan Odden and colleagues recently compiled a review of research that attempts to quantify the impact of different strategies for improving student performance. Only two of these individual attention strategies— class-size reduction and tutoring—have significant bodies of research to allow summary of estimated effect size (Odden et al., 2006). The authors explained that "effect size" measures how much higher student proficiency scores rise with the specific strategy. An effect size of 0.25 measures as statistically significant, and 0.5 is "substantial." An effect size of 1.0 would mean that the average student scoring at the 50th percentile would rise to the 83rd percentile. Looking at the numbers in Figure 4.2, the effect size is not dramatic for a class-size reduction. However, the findings do suggest a wide range of impact from individual tutoring. This wide range of effectiveness makes sense because there are so many different ways to implement a tutoring strategy.

Figure 4.2 Effect size of individual attention strategies

Strategy	Effect Size
Class Size of 15 in Grades K–3 • Overall • Low-income and minority students	0.25 0.5
One-to-One Tutoring	0.4–2.5

SOURCE: From *An Evidence-Based Approach to School Finance Adequacy in Washington*, by A. Odden, L. Picus, M. Goetz, and M. Fermanich, 2006, Hollywood, CA: Lawrence O. Picus and Associates. Reprinted with permission.

Because class-size reduction is not the only option for school leaders to consider for creating individual attention, we are careful to use the phrase "small-group sizes" as we articulate this principle of individual attention. In his seminal work, *The Culture of the School and the Problem of Change*, Seymour Sarason (1971/1982) wrote:

> The fact is that one of the major factors maximizing the gulf between educational goals and accomplishments has been the way resources have been defined . . . There is a universe of alternatives one can consider and if we do not confront the universe, it is largely because we are committed to a way of defining who should be in the classroom . . . One teacher to one classroom is not an end in itself, but one means of providing more time for individual students when needed. (p. 277)

As we have emphasized throughout this book, no single strategy can account for improved student performance. Instead, the way schools combine these strategies to fit student needs and match teacher capacity determines their effectiveness—and this is what sets higher-performing schools apart. We'll turn first to grouping strategies in elementary schools and then discuss secondary school strategies.

Student-Teacher Groupings in Elementary Schools

Typical elementary schools tend to use class size, flexible grouping, and tutoring strategies in very consistent ways, as shown in Figure 4.3.

The typical staffing pattern described in Figure 4.4 results in an interesting situation in most schools, where the overall number of students for each instructor looks very different than average class sizes. Figure 4.4, an example from an urban school we have worked with, provides a way of quantifying the impact of specialization.

In this example, regular class sizes average 25. When Title I teachers are added to the mix, the schoolwide student-teacher ratio drops to 23. If resource room teachers are added, the ratio drops further to 21. Adding students and teachers assigned to self-contained special-education classes reduces the ratio to 19.5. Finally, including the art, music, and physical-education teachers brings the ratio for the schoolwide average to one teacher for every 18 students. One teacher for every 18 students looks and feels very different than the perceived one for every 25 and may open up new possibilities. In Chapter 6, we walk through the method for performing these calculations for your own school. Although this way of organizing resources outside the regular classroom works well for many schools,

Figure 4.3 Student-teacher groupings in typical versus strategic elementary schools

Practice	Typical Elementary School	Strategic Elementary School
Class size	• Size ranges from 18–25, often lower in K–3. • Regular education classes are roughly the same size regardless of student need. • Specialist classes are roughly the same size as regular-education classes. • Some schools separate students into classes by ability.	• Reduce class size in high-priority areas such as early grades, reading, and math.
Flexible grouping	• Students who need extra support are pulled out of class for special instruction. • Most classes use small reading groups but otherwise instruct class as a whole. • Many small groups stay together for the year and do not change based on student progress.	• Create small groups that are flexible and change based on subject and student progress. • Use other adults from the school building to come into classrooms and provide support during flexible-group time.
Individual tutoring	• Because of its high expense, typical schools do not have enough resources to provide tutoring to all students who could benefit from it. • If they do have tutoring, it seems to be an inconsistent and short-lived event, sometimes even competing with content from the regular classroom.	• Tutoring is integrated into homeroom's regular instruction and curriculum. • Students may work with a tutor regularly until they no longer need the services.

the resources have become almost hidden, and school leaders may not realize the resources they have for alternative strategies.

Strategic schools find a host of ways to create smaller learning groups that match their most expert resources to the learning needs of students and focus especially on the early grades, literacy, and math. Their choices depend on the set of resources they have to work with, their teacher capacity, and the mix of student needs they have. They combine three elementary

Figure 4.4   Student-teacher ratios in a prototypical elementary school

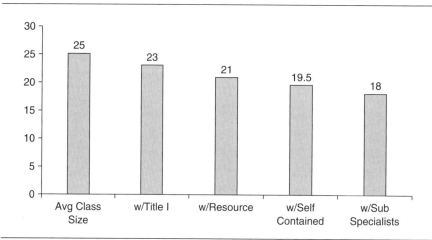

school–level strategies described previously (class size, flexible grouping, and individual tutoring) to respond to assessed student skill levels.

Class Size. As we have discussed, the research suggests that significant class-size reductions in the earliest grades can be a powerful, although expensive, strategy. When resources permit, the high-performing schools we have studied create dramatically reduced class sizes. For example, the Mary Lyon school in Boston, which has a high population of intensive-needs special-education students, integrates all students and teaching staff together to create class sizes of 15, each with an assistant teacher who is working toward a master's degree in special education. The Mary Lyon strategy clearly recognizes that reduced class size does not lead to improved achievement unless teachers have the skills to make effective use of smaller group sizes to meet individual needs. Because the Mary Lyon strategy integrates students with special needs into the regular-education classroom, all teachers at Mary Lyon have or are working toward their special-education certification.

Flexible, Skill-Based Grouping. Because we studied schools that work within the typical level of public school resources, we did not find that most high-performing schools implemented across-the-board class-size reductions. In fact, they sometimes raise average class size to free resources for more strategic ways of providing individual attention for all students based on skill. Although the research suggests that "tracking" students—putting them into semi-permanent groups based on ability—can be harmful, it is also clear that adapting curriculum, pacing, and instructional strategies to more closely match student skill levels can benefit low performers *and* high-performing students (Allington & Cunningham, 2002; Loveless, 1998; Slavin, 1995). We call this set of strategies "flexible, skill-based grouping."

Skill-based grouping differs from tracking because it requires teachers to continuously assess each student's skills by subject and then to create and re-create small, flexible groups for reading and math. Grouping should vary by subject and change regularly based on student progress. Skill-based grouping, especially in the early elementary years, has the explicit purpose of ensuring that students who are missing important skills or knowledge gain them and, whenever possible, move to the next skill level. As an example, Henry Levin (1991) has devised a widespread, comprehensive reform model called Accelerated Learning, in which students who are behind in literacy or math receive extra support so that they rejoin their peers as quickly as possible. (For more information on Accelerated Learning, visit www.acceleratedlearning.com.)

The most effective teachers routinely create small groups within their own classrooms to tailor instruction more closely to student needs. When researchers compare accomplished teachers of early reading with those who are least effective, they note that the least effective teachers spend only 25 minutes per day in small reading groups, whereas the most accomplished teachers spend 48 minutes per day—almost double the time—in small literacy groups (J. Murphy, 2004; Taylor & Taxis, 1999).

Most schools have enough resources to provide additional expert support for teacher-facilitated small-group instruction in reading and literacy in the earliest grades. The Dever Elementary School in Boston, Massachusetts, leverages all teachers in the building to reduce class size during its daily, 90-minute literacy block, in a model they call Literacy Support Teams. To reduce class sizes from 25 to 28 students down to 12 to 18 students per teacher, each classroom teacher co-teaches with a specialist. To achieve even smaller groupings, specialist resource teachers and two literacy specialists rotate into the classrooms. All of these teachers receive training in the school's literacy model, and several specialists also take literacy courses at the local teacher's college (Shields, 1999). The Dever strategy is similar to the standard strategy prescribed by the Success for All model, in which all teachers are trained to teach reading and students are regrouped for reading into smaller groups based on assessed skill level. Teaching teams review students' assessment results with the literacy facilitator every six weeks to identify whether a student needs individual tutoring to continue progressing or whether he or she has progressed so far that the student should move to the next skill level.

Another strategy for creating small learning groups for reading uses highly trained reading specialists to team with regular classroom teachers during reading periods to create small group sizes and provide individual attention. Quebec Heights Elementary School in Cincinnati improved student reading scores by using three highly trained reading specialists to rotate through the classrooms during reading periods scheduled throughout the day. The specialists enabled teacher-facilitated group sizes for reading of eight or fewer in all classrooms every day for reading (Miles & Darling-Hammond, 1997). Oak Grove Elementary School in California raised reading scores by hiring a cadre of part-time expert reading teachers who went into homeroom classrooms on a defined schedule from 9 a.m. to 1 p.m. each day. This doubled the number of teachers who could work with students in small groups and also allowed group sizes of eight or fewer. Both schools funded this strategy by increasing homeroom classes slightly to provide targeted specialists.

Although the previous examples focus on creating small, skill-based groups for literacy, the same strategies can also be used to target individual attention in math. Finding ways to target expert individual attention in math can be especially important because studies have shown that many elementary school teachers do not feel as confident in their math skills as in literacy (Nelson & Landel, 2006; Wenglinsky & Silverstein, 2006). Nelson and Landel (2006) described a "collaborative" specialist model that has the effect of building teacher capacity and ensuring students have expert support in math. In this model, highly-trained teachers in a subject area such as science team with regular classroom teachers during the math period to provide more customized instruction.

Tutoring. Tutoring provides a final strategy for reducing group sizes. As summarized previously, one-on-one tutoring by a trained professional is one of the most powerful and potentially effective ways to instruct a student. However, because it is also the most resource intensive, tutoring is typically only considered an appropriate intervention for students who are significantly behind grade level. Wasik and Slavin (1993) summarized studies of five thoughtfully designed tutoring methods: Reading Recovery, Success for All, the Wallach Tutoring program, Prevention of Learning Disabilities, and Programmed Tutorial Reading. These successful programs differ both in design and in influence, offering different reading models, different curricula, and varying amounts of tutoring. The most successful of these tutoring programs share two common characteristics:

- they incorporate comprehensive models of reading with a more complete set of instructional interventions, and
- they use certified or highly trained instructors rather than paraprofessionals.

The most successful single program, Success for All, includes tutoring that is closely integrated with the ongoing classroom activities and approach (Wasik & Slavin, 1993). Because tutoring is so expensive, it must be used sparingly and in connection with other classroom strategies, including flexible grouping. We assert that tutoring will be most effective at bringing all students to standard when it is explicitly integrated with the homeroom's instructional curriculum and approach and when students become eligible for specific tutoring activities based on ongoing assessment results rather than a once-annual programmatic categorization.

A Blended Approach: The Family Model. The Children's School of Rochester (CSR), New York, provides an example of how a school might combine these concepts and strategies to create small homeroom class sizes along with specialized small-group instruction based on student needs. CSR has achieved significant student performance gains, in part, by eliminating the concept of one teacher per classroom (Carlisle, Litt, & Shields, 2006). CSR is roughly similar demographically to other schools in Rochester. Sixty-eight percent of this school's 300 students qualify for free or reduced-price lunch, 45% are English language learners, and 8% have been diagnosed with special needs. However, the CSR's performance in recent years has been exceptional. In a district in which three out of five children do not meet state literacy standards, more than 90% of the children in the CSR met these standards in 2004, and pass rates have climbed each year. CSR students have achieved similar results in math, and they exceed district averages on other performance measures such as attendance.

To achieve this success without receiving extra resources, CSR eliminated one-teacher classrooms in favor of family groups of 45 students that each have three teachers. These teacher teams use a full-inclusion model that serves all special-education and English language learning (ELL) students as well as regular-education students. Each team includes a special-education, ELL, or subject specialist (math or literacy) teacher. To promote accountability and stability for students, each teacher in the family has a primary assignment or "home base" of 15 students. This class size of 15 is close to the district average and is not created by any special allocation, but all teachers work with all students, and there are no limits placed on how much time students spend with a specific teacher. The daily schedule is entirely flexible and allows any number of grouping opportunities throughout a given day at the discretion of the three teachers. Figure 4.5 shows how this might work with a student-teacher ratio of 15 to 1.

To determine who will be working with whom, on what, and for how long, the CSR teachers use daily collaboration time and an extensive system of daily formative assessments, in which they use a formal protocol with a rubric to observe how each student is engaging with assigned

Figure 4.5   Children's School of Rochester family grouping strategy

Family Grouping Strategy Example
From Three Classrooms of 15:1 → To Family Groups of 45:3

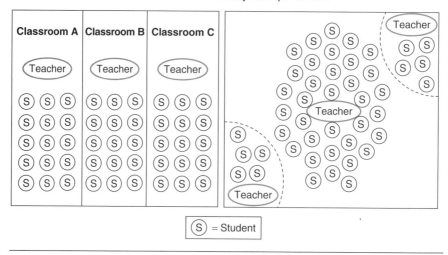

work. Often, one teacher conducts large-group instruction for most students while the other two teachers conduct small-group or tutoring sessions as they deem appropriate. This schedule allows the teachers to decide how important it is for certain students to engage with various subjects as well as to experiment with group sizes. Together, teachers can identify students who may be struggling with a particular reading or math concept and support them before they fall behind the rest of the class. To be successful, this type of flexible grouping system requires formative assessments to be fully integrated into the continuous daily activities of students and teachers.

In the course of our work with district reformers, we are frequently reminded that structural reforms such as those described in this chapter only succeed when they improve the quality of instruction students receive, which depends on the initial capacity and skill of the teachers and type of professional development provided. Successfully integrating special-education and other supplemental resources into the classroom presupposes that teachers have (or are supported in acquiring) the capability, knowledge, and skills to do what we ask of them. Yet we find the structural reforms we discuss here particularly exciting precisely because research on highly effective teachers indicates that they (a) spend far more time with students in flexible groups, (b) are more likely to collaborate with their fellow teachers, and (c) attend religiously to formative assessments. In short, the structures described here virtually require teachers to engage in the very activities that appear to make teachers more effective (J. Murphy, 2004; Taylor & Taxis, 1999).

Grouping Strategies in Typical Secondary Schools

Creating individual attention at the secondary school level takes different forms and challenges for three primary reasons.

First, most secondary schools organize by subject area, making individual attention and a sense of community and relationships significantly harder to achieve. As Figure 4.6 shows, at the elementary school level, students and teachers are grouped for most of the day in group sizes between 20 and 30. At the secondary school level, class sizes typically rise, and teachers see four to six class groups of students per day (and sometimes even more than that per year). At the same time, the cohort that students interact with grows exponentially as well; now students must get to know at least four new teachers and interact with a cohort of as many as 100 different students in a day depending on how classes are scheduled. Second, teenagers are in a different stage of social-emotional development than elementary students and are more likely to challenge authority or to demand that lessons relate to their daily lives in readily apparent ways.

Third, by the time students reach secondary school, they display a more diverse set of academic needs. Some have excelled beyond their grade level while others have lagged behind.

The same set of strategies for providing individual attention around content areas exists at the secondary school level as at the elementary school level: reducing class size, grouping in smaller flexible groups for skill-based instruction, and providing individual tutoring. However, subject specialization adds a different twist. First, because teachers see so many more classes each day, the importance of strategically managing teacher-student load is increased. Second, because classes are already separated by subject area, there are opportunities for more targeted reduction in class sizes by subject area. We focus on class size and teacher-student load in the following (see Figure 4.7).

Figure 4.6   Why personalization decreases from elementary to secondary school

Elementary School	Secondary School
Students see • 20 other students during core classes • 1–2 teachers in core classes	Students see • 100–150+ other students during core classes • 3–4 teachers in core classes
Core teachers see • 20–30 students for most of the day	Core teachers see • 120–160 students each for small parts of the day

Figure 4.7   Student-teacher groupings in typical versus strategic secondary schools

Practice	Typical Secondary School	Strategic Secondary School
Class size	• Class size is the same in all core subjects. • Class size in electives varies depending on enrollment.	• Class size in core subjects varies by grade and subject purposefully to address student needs. • Class size in electives is managed to maximize enrollment.
Teacher load	• Teachers are responsible for more than 100 students in core subjects.	• There is some evidence of targeted reduction of teacher load in some subjects and grades.
Flexible grouping and individual tutoring	• This is limited.	• This is more systematic to address particular student needs.

Class Size. There is limited research on the effect of reducing class size on secondary school student performance (Miles, Shields, & City, 2007). However, given the research at the elementary level, we might make two safe predictions. First, it might make sense that small reductions in class size would have less impact than much larger reductions. Second, even large reductions in class size can only be effective when there is also a strategy to change instruction in a way that takes advantage of the smaller class sizes.

We have examined class sizes in thousands of schools in districts across the country and find that most staffing and time decisions in secondary schools are driven by graduation requirements and practical considerations—not by student need for smaller classes or increased individual attention. Instead of organizing to provide individual attention in core academic classrooms, secondary schools typically have similar class sizes across all subjects—both core and elective. In fact, we often find that class sizes for electives are *lower* than those in academic subjects.

Figure 4.8 shows summary data from a typical district with which we have worked. In this particular example, a majority of the high-poverty students served are multiple years behind standards in reading, prompting the school district to state publicly that literacy is the primary focus of its secondary improvement efforts. And yet we see English/language arts class sizes that, at 26, are as high as any other core academic subject and higher than all noncore academic subjects except physical education.

Figure 4.8   District "X" average class size by subject: Secondary schools

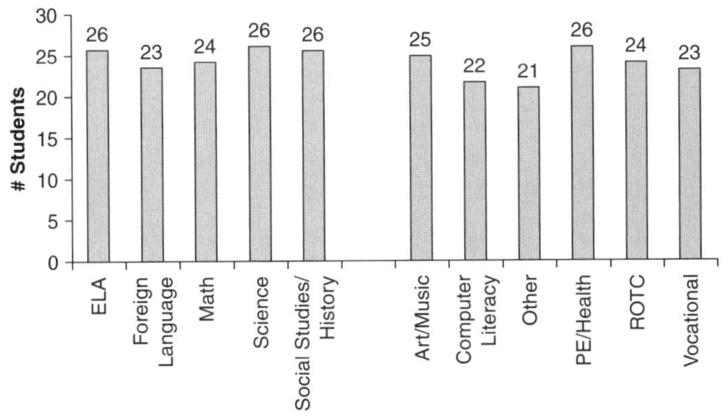

NOTE: ELA = English/language arts; PE = physical education.

When we analyze class sizes by grade, we most often find that class sizes decrease steadily from ninth through twelfth grades. School leaders we work with are frequently surprised by this finding. In one district, the superintendent had just spent millions of dollars to create ninth-grade academies through shifted investment toward ninth-grade students. When we explored resource use more deeply, we found that despite efforts, upperclass students still experienced significantly lower class sizes and thus higher levels of investment. The most important explanation for this is that as students finish their required core courses, they begin to take elective classes that fewer and fewer students take (e.g., French III and IV). When schools offer a wide range of advanced or upperclass electives, a laudable goal in many situations, then the typical tradeoff is that their twelfth-grade elective classes will cost far more than their ninth-grade core classes—due to smaller class sizes.

Teacher Load. One of the most important indicators of the *potential* for individual attention in secondary schools is the teacher's student count, sometimes called a "teacher load." Conceptually, a teacher load refers to how many students a teacher teaches in a given time period.[1] Lower teacher loads allow greater opportunity to build relationships between teachers and students. Teachers who see 50 students per week have a

1. In some schedules, the number of students seen each week (weekly student count) differs significantly from the number of students seen each year (annual student count). Although both concepts are important, we discuss the weekly student count here to show its greater effect on whether teachers have enough time to meaningfully assess the assignments of all of their students.

better chance of really knowing students personally and academically and tailoring their instruction accordingly than teachers who teach 125 students per week. Although there are no large-scale statistical studies to point to, a preponderance of anecdotal and case evidence suggests that teacher load impacts instruction a great deal (Miles et al., 2007).

The weekly teacher load helps determine how much time a teacher must devote to grading student work. The contracted time that teachers have to devote to this is typically quite small and may be insufficient to consistently make meaningful adjustments for specific students when loads are high. Swaim and Swaim (1999) showed how challenging it can be for teachers to plan for classes and grade papers when the weekly teaching load is 125 students. According to their calculations, for a typical teacher to spend 12 minutes preparing for each lesson and only 9 minutes per week grading homework assignments per student, teachers must work at least 60 hours per week regardless of how many (or few) hours the teacher contract pays them for (Swaim & Swaim, 1999). Giving the current emphasis on improving critical thinking and demonstrating this through writing, it seems hard to imagine that teachers might effectively respond to student writing with fewer than 10 minutes per week to review student work.

Ted Sizer (1992), in his eloquent description of *Horace's Compromise*, documented why it is clearly impossible for even the best secondary teachers to diagnose the needs of most of their students when the teacher load is high (and we typically see the load range from 130 to 160 students per day). To cope with such a large number of students, Horace simplifies assignments, reduces the number and length of assignments, spends less time grading assignments and providing feedback, and reluctantly relies on previously prepared class materials even when he knows that they don't quite meet the needs of the current group of students. As the list goes on, Horace's compromises make him a less effective teacher, contribute to feelings of guilt and inadequacy, and gradually decrease his own motivation.

Schools can reduce the number of students teachers have responsibility for in three primary ways:

1. Reducing the number of periods each teacher teaches per day— four out of six periods instead of five out of six for example. This strategy reduces the percentage of time teachers spend in instruction and so adds significant cost.

2. Combining subjects to create longer periods, so one period of English becomes a two-period block that includes both English and social studies. In this example, teachers become responsible for student learning in two subjects but have half the number of students.

3. Semesterizing (or trimesterizing) to lengthen the time spent on the subject each day but teaching it only part of the year, so a student might take science for a double period each day for a semester, and the next semester, a student would take history instead. In this example, the teacher has half the weekly load but the same annual load.

We explore several examples of schools that have dramatically reduced teacher load using these strategies in our discussion of high-performing secondary schools in the following.

Student-Teacher Groupings in High-Performing Secondary Schools

High-performing schools use two primary strategies for creating smaller group sizes: targeted and dramatic reductions in class size and lowering teacher load to create more personal learning environments.

Targeted and Dramatic Reductions in Class Size. High-performing schools prioritize their opportunities for individual attention based on student needs. For example, some schools create small groups and class sizes for specific groups of students with high needs, such as students in a transition year (first year of middle or high school), ELL students, students who are performing below grade level in reading or math, or other students who may be at risk of failing or dropping out of school.

Others create greater opportunities for small group size or individual attention by focusing on core academic areas students must master before leaving school—often literacy and math. Although it tends to be prohibitively expensive for schools to reduce class sizes globally, many schools find that they can free the resources to dramatically reduce class sizes in one priority subject, especially for a subgroup of struggling students. They often fund these reductions in part by raising class sizes in other subjects.

The Raphael Hernandez School, a PreK–8 School in Boston, Massachusetts, wanted to lower its class size during its daily, 90-minute literacy block. A Spanish bilingual school, Hernandez receives a paraprofessional for every bilingual class with more than 18 students (Shields, 1999). During literacy blocks, these paraprofessionals come into the classroom to support the larger class as students complete their computer work or writing activities. At the same time, the regular teacher leads small groups in literacy lessons. This arrangements allows literacy group size to lower in all grades (Grades K–3 sizes are 5 to 6 students, Grades 4–5 sizes are 10 to 12 students, and Grades 6 and 8 small-group sizes are 9 to 10 students). The school includes paraprofessionals in its literacy training classes to ensure they have the capacity to support students effectively. The school also uses a full-time literacy specialist, a reading recovery teacher, and literacy volunteers to support students during this time.

In another example, the Boston Arts Academy (BAA), an arts and college-preparation high school in Boston, Massachusetts, describes its mission as "being a laboratory and a beacon for artistic and academic innovation" (Shields & Miles, 2008). BAA students major in music, dance, visual arts, or theatre and pursue courses in humanities, math, science, writing, and foreign language. BAA strives to personalize teaching and learning for all students. One way BAA achieves this goal is having low teacher loads and small class sizes, especially in core academic classes. Humanities and math teachers have a low teacher load of about 35 students each semester and a teacher load of 70 students for the year (excluding writing and advisory). Because BAA teachers believe writing must be practiced year round, students take a yearlong writing seminar in groups of 10 students. To accomplish this grouping, all teachers and school professionals have writing seminar responsibilities. BAA conducts professional development for all teachers regardless of subject in writing and pairs teachers together for the seminar (two teachers for 20 students) to promote sharing of practice and ensure each group has a more-expert writing teacher. This practice allows teachers to come to know students through their academic work and to devote significant time to working individually with them (Shields & Miles, 2008).

Lowering Teacher Load to Create More Personal Learning Environments. High-performing schools find ways to reduce teacher load, particularly in targeted subjects and at the middle school level, where combining subjects for instruction is easier because teachers don't need to master as advanced a skill set as at high levels of math and science, for example.

Harrison Place High School used teacher load as a tool for improved student performance. After the 1988–1989 school year, Harrison Place High School was forced to close due to ongoing poor performance. Reopening in 1989, the school transformed itself and now places in the highest category for academic performance in the district. Before restructuring, the school had a seven-period day, with students taking academic classes for four of those periods. Class size was 30 to 1, and teacher load was 120. Since reallocating its resources to focus on academics, the school has reduced its class size to 18 to 1 and adopted an eight-period day with two long, 135-minute blocks for core academic subjects—one English/language arts/social studies and one science/math. This schedule allows teachers to spend more time with a smaller number of students, reducing teacher load from 120 to 80 (Archibald, 2001).

Another example is New York's Central Park East Secondary School, which serves 450 students in Grades 7 through 12, about 25% of whom qualified for special education and 60% for free or reduced-price lunch. This high-performing school deliberately allocates nearly all of its positions for teaching, rather than hiring guidance counselors and various administrative staff, to reduce academic class sizes (Miles & Darling-Hammond, 1997). Furthermore, except for two special-education teachers, the only teachers on staff teach one of two core subjects—humanities or math/science. Adjunct or part-time staff teach all other subjects. This reduces core academic class sizes to about 18 heterogeneously grouped students. Although the class-size reduction does lower teaching load, the more leveraged factor is that the students in Grades 7 to 10 are scheduled for two, two-hour academic courses each day, humanities and math/science plus a foreign language offered in a shorter period before school. All full-time teachers in these grades, with the exception of two special-education resource room teachers, teach one of the two interdisciplinary courses. This gave Central Park East's Grade 7 to 10 teachers a load of 36 students—almost 100 students *fewer* than the typical schools described previously (Miles & Darling-Hammond, 1998).

Particularly possible at the middle-grade level, innovative types of block scheduling can reduce teacher load dramatically even when the budget for class-size reduction does not exist. For instance, if Central Park East had adopted this schedule with class sizes of 28, teacher load would have dropped from more than 130 down to 56.

Individual Attention Principle G:
Organizing Structures That Foster Personal
Relationships Between Students and Teachers

When teachers relate well to students, feedback becomes more meaningful, examples more relevant, tasks and activities more engaging, and opportunities for self-directed study more plentiful. Healthy relationships foster mutual accountability for learning and inspire both parties to expand their attendance, preparation, and effort. We identify three categories of structures that increase the possibility for strong relationships that support community and learning and help ensure that students do not "get lost" in larger schools. These include

- **Advocates.** Structures and strategies that try to build a deep relationship between the student and (usually) one faculty advocate or advisor who is responsible for understanding the child's academic and nonacademic needs and actively works to ensure student success, however defined.

- **Communities.** Structures that try to promote a sense of identifiable community, often by limiting the number of students and teachers students interact with regularly. Examples include clusters, teams, small learning communities, and small schools.
- **Looping.** Strategy for keeping students and teachers together for two or three years in high-need subjects or critical grade junctures.

These structures surround and support the individual attention strategies described previously and should be designed in relationship to them. They are much more important at the secondary school level, where teacher loads make individual attention and relationships around content more difficult. In addition, elementary schools tend to be significantly smaller than secondary schools, so that strategies for creating smaller communities are less important.

Advocates

Many schools assign each student an advocate as a key strategy for ensuring that students have relationships with adults who can actively support them through high school and beyond. Traditionally, guidance counselors play this role. However, the guidance counselor job description limits counselors' advocacy role. First, counselors are often assigned more than 300 students—a number that inherently prohibits the development of a deep, one-on-one relationship with each student. Second, counselors are divorced from the teaching and content of the students' classrooms, making it more difficult to truly understand the learning needs of each individual student. These factors often reduce the counselors to checking credits and filling out applications, writing references for students they barely know, or responding to crises long after they have occurred.

"Advisories"—small groups of students who meet with an adult regularly for the purpose of fostering relationships—have become a popular structure for addressing the shortcomings of the guidance counselor role. Schools implement advisory programs with objectives as varied as building relationships, constructing a group identity, providing developmental guidance, improving academic performance, or providing simple relaxation (Osofsky, Sinner, & Wolk, 2003). However, in our observations, schools often implement advisories without paying enough attention to the content or the quality of the interactions that take place in the advisory period. The purpose behind the program can become lost behind the structure, and the advisory becomes little more than an extended home-room period. Without support or training, teachers begin to resent the additional responsibility, and the program can lose effectiveness. In other cases, the advisory program takes the place of other personalization strategies and can lessen the sense of urgency for creating individual attention in the core academic areas.

High-performing schools are more deliberate in their use of advisory and how it fits with their other individual attention strategies. They design curricula to provide support matched to student need at different stages. For instance, as students get closer to graduation, the focus might shift toward college or career preparation. The Education Alliance at Brown University suggests five keys to running successful advisory programs (Osofsky et al., 2003):

- A stated purpose
- Thoughtful organization
- Relevant advisory program content
- Ongoing assessment
- Strong leadership

Many schools we have worked with eliminate the guidance counselor role entirely and use the advisory structure instead, reasoning that the traditional guidance counselor role of planning a program of study, supporting college applications, and providing social and emotional support is better provided by an individual with a smaller caseload who knows the student because of regular work with him or her. For this strategy to work, teachers need to commit to playing this role and may need support in using this time effectively. As way of acknowledging the teacher commitment involved, Central Park East School in New York City asked teachers to sign a memorandum of understanding that stated that they agreed to play this role in the context of the low teaching loads (36) and significant planning time that came with a teaching job at Central Park East (Miles & Darling-Hammond, 1997).

The advisory program at Life Academy, a small biosciences high school in Oakland, California, illustrates how a high school can create an advisory structure that reinforces its school design and complements the other ways that students receive individual attention in their school. Life Academy's advisory program has two purposes—to build individual relationships with students and provide additional academic support in literacy. Every adult at Life Academy has an advisory group, including the administrators. Students stay with the same advisor for four years, allowing staff to get to know students and their families and support student learning throughout the students' high school experience. Advisory classes include students from all grades, with 16 to 18 students in each class. The classes meet each morning for five minutes to check in before class and then for an additional 50 minutes four times per week. Students read in advisory twice each week and spend the other sessions on academic support and social issues. The time devoted to literacy through advisory results in an extra 57 hours of reading enrichment for all students per year. The advisory curriculum is planned by the committee and shared with the staff so teachers are not burdened by the planning.

The advisory program at Life Academy was originally designed to have students switch advisors each year, but the school found that the consistency of the relationships with students increased the level of personalization in addition to fostering ongoing relationships with families (Shields & Miles, 2008).

Communities

Community structures break faculty and students into smaller groups that share some kind of identity and common work. These strategies range from creating teacher teams that share a common group of students in a school to breaking large schools into small, completely self-contained schools with their own budgets and leadership.

As with advocacy structures, too often, typical schools do not couple these larger structural moves with the deeper changes in practice, instruction, and philosophy that create more individual attention and stronger relationships. For example, a teacher team that shared the same set of students for math and science would have the potential to collaborate to understand and support individual students. They could also work together to plan lessons that would reinforce each other and respond to difficulties or passions of the student group. They might even choose to combine their classrooms for some lessons or time periods depending on the purpose. But doing this requires a master schedule that supports this teacher collaboration with sufficient team time for teachers and schedules the shared classes sequentially or at the same time. Also, teachers need to commit to working together as a team and might need support to begin to do this. Likewise, creating a school or learning community that is small in size does not ensure that students will feel more known by teachers who see 150 students each day.

High-performing schools that use learning communities implement them purposely to complement the academic program and vision. The Graham and Parks Middle school in Cambridge, Massachusetts, uses teacher teaming, small size, and looping to create community as well as shared accountability for student performance. A teacher team of four shares the school's entire cohort of seventh and eighth graders—between 75 and 80 each year. Two of these teachers teach a double-period block (85 minutes) of humanities to two groups of seventh and eighth graders per day with a teaching load of 36 to 40 students each year. Students and teachers remain together through both years, which is called looping. The math and science teachers each teach separate seventh- and eighth-grade classes and have loads of 75. However, because they teach students for two years, this enables them to know students deeply (see www.cpsd .us/GAP/index.cfm).

Graham and Parks teachers instruct students for four out of six periods each day, with two periods free each day for collaborative planning time and "community meetings." Collaborative time happens three times a week, and teachers use it to work together to address student issues, create curriculum, and meet in student-support teams. Three times a month, students and teachers meet together in "community meetings," where they receive leadership training, collaborate to do group problem solving, and initiate community service activities. The combination of strategies— structural individualization strategies like school size, looping, and teacher teaming along with curriculum, philosophy, teacher load changes, and scheduling—create a powerful whole.

Looping

Looping structures provide a way to create deeper relationships and increase individual attention. Looping refers to the practice of keeping students with the same teacher for more than one year. Looping, although potentially powerful, is rarely used in elementary schools, because in most schools this would require that teachers become expert across all subject areas for two grades. Yearly testing at each grade level has made this strategy difficult to implement. At the secondary school level, looping seems to occur most often by happenstance rather than as a coherent strategy for expanded interaction with core academic teachers. For example, perhaps in a small school when the same teacher teaches algebra and geometry, students might loop and have the same math teacher for two years.

Benefits to looping include teachers and students knowing each other more and saving instructional time because the teacher can pick up building on where the student ended the previous year. However, looping can be extremely challenging to implement and requires changes to other school structures. For example, teachers may need professional development to teach a different grade level or need a higher number of preparation periods to plan across multiple subjects.

Several high-performing schools that we have studied use looping strategies to support their goals. Quebec Heights Elementary School in Cincinnati, Ohio, is a K–6 school that structured its students into family clusters of 75 to 85 students and three to four teachers (Miles & Darling-Hammond, 1997). Each family looped together for three years to build stronger relationships and ensure continuity across years, especially in math and science instruction. Each student has a homeroom class of about 22 students, and this teacher has primary responsibility for the student. However, students move to different teachers through the day depending on this lesson. Teachers in Grades 4 through 6 "departmentalized," with two teachers teaching math and science. This helped them to address the very significant challenge of needing to teach different content across three grade levels.

Perspectives Charter School in Chicago, serving Grades 6 to 12, loops its students and teachers for two years. This means that a ninth-grade student will have the same content teachers in tenth grade, and an eleventh-grade student will have the same content teachers in twelfth grade. This looping strategy enables teachers to build a relationship with their students and get to know each student's learning style. Teachers are then able to take this understanding of individual students and meet in grade-based teams to discuss student progress. The looping structure also allows students to move in a cohort of classmates for two consecutive years, also fostering the feeling of smallness within the school through a personalized learning environment (Shields & Miles, 2008).

Looking across these strategies for creating individual attention—assessing student learning, creating smaller group sizes, and fostering personal relationships—it becomes clear that structures that promote interactions will only be effective when teachers and students know how to use those interactions effectively and responsibly to create goodwill and accountability for teaching and learning. Creating individual attention is not something that can be done by checking off a laundry list—the more programs you have, the better your individual attention. Rather, successful schools will pick a strategy for providing individual attention that takes into account their curriculum, performance goals, faculty experience, knowledge, and skills, and the amount of resources available. In most cases, it is not the presence or absence of a specific factor (such as low or high class sizes) that is important but rather the confluence of a range of factors that work together to ensure that each student is given the educational experiences he or she needs to flourish.

Maximizing Academic Time and Linking It to Learning Needs

5

As the old saying goes, time is money. In the case of school resources, the impact of time extends beyond money. It affects what and how much is taught and learned, how much teachers collaborate, and how frequently and thoroughly they assess student progress. Its influence is pervasive, affecting all activities in a school. Of the hundreds of principals we have talked to on the subject of time, nearly all wish for more of it. Some want more time to create a longer literacy block. Others wish they could require an additional period of math or English. Others want more time to provide character building or community outreach activities.

How much time is available? On average, U.S. students spend between 1,000 and 1,200 hours per year in school (Education Resource Strategies, 2006; National Education Commission on Time and Learning, 1994). However, available time varies greatly across schools and districts driven by state education and school funding policies, union contracts, and other factors. Although the number of days per year (180 +/− 6 days) is similar in most districts and states, the number of hours per day is not. For example, when we studied the length of student days across the 10 largest urban districts in the United States, we found that Chicago Public School students spend slightly more than five hours per day for 180 days in school, for a meager total of 940 hours in school each year. By contrast, Houston and Philadelphia students spend more than seven hours per day in school, or more than 1,250 annual hours. All told, the annual calendars of Houston and Philadelphia contain more than 30% more hours than the Chicago calendar. As a result, Chicago students spend the equivalent of eight fewer weeks in class than most of their other urban counterparts every year (Miles & Frank, 2006).

Researchers have questioned whether U.S. schools have enough time to do all that we ask of them. In 1995, for instance, results from the Third International Math and Science Study of 41 countries suggested that a primary reason American students fall behind other countries' students by the eleventh grade is because our students spend less time in highly demanding subjects (Schmidt, McKnight, & Raizen, 1996). Others suggest that U.S. standards and curriculum are too broad and that "as the school year is currently structured, schooling would have to be extended from kindergarten to grade 21 or 22 to accommodate all the standards and benchmarks in the national documents" (Marzano, 2003).

These and related criticisms of time in U.S. public schools have prompted reform efforts to increase the amount of time in the school year, including statewide legislative initiatives, citywide pilot programs, and charter and school design models built around the principle of increased learning time. On the other hand, the research is clear that extending the school day must be done together with increasing high-quality instruction (WestEd, 1998). Research consistently demonstrates that when students are held to high standards and taught well, more academic instructional time *does* raise student achievement (Sheerens & Bosker, 1997). In particular, schools that devote more time to literacy and math and use this time well show dramatic improvements in student achievement (Education Trust, 1999). Not surprisingly, researchers have also found that adding more time to the school day when it is used ineffectively has *not* been shown to have much impact on student performance and can be extraordinarily expensive (WestEd, 1998). It is especially costly when schools attempt to increase the school year for all students regardless of need.

Because time is expensive, before lobbying for additional time, school leaders first need to ask themselves: How are we using the time we already have? Can we reallocate our time to better support our school's goals and design?

We have argued that rigid structures wrought by our historical legacy adhere to U.S. schools with a pervasive rigor. We cling to our misuse of time with especial tenacity. The recently re-released study *Prisoners of Time* concludes once again that

- secondary students in "other post-industrial countries" spend twice as much time on instruction in core academics than their U.S. counterparts;
- in the 42 states included in the study, only 41% of secondary school time is spent in core academics; and

- on average, schools divide their day into 51-minute periods regardless of the complexity or mastery of the subject (National Education Commission on Time and Learning, 1994).

In other words, both elementary and secondary schools allocate their time in much the same way as they have for the last 50 years despite research that suggests that the factory model of school scheduling—nine-month years, 60-minute periods—is obsolete (Time, Learning, and Afterschool Task Force, 2007).

HOW STRATEGIC SCHOOLS MAXIMIZE THE TIME THEY SPEND ON CORE ACADEMICS AND LINK IT TO LEARNING NEEDS

By contrast, the high-performing schools we studied almost universally keep to two principles with regard to academic time by

H. Maximizing time, including longer blocks of uninterrupted time, that students spend on academic subjects

I. Varying time and instructional programs to ensure all students meet rigorous academic standards

Before we explore these two principles in detail, we need a framework for evaluating how schools use time.

A Framework for Evaluating How Time Is Used in Schools

How do we begin thinking about whether time is used for academic learning in schools? Researchers have proposed a variety of frameworks for thinking about time use (see, for instance, Roth, Brooks-Gunn, Linver, & Hofferth, 2003; Silva, 2007). Although the details and language may differ slightly, the overall concept is similar. Elena Silva's (2007) work in *On the Clock* gives us a framework by which to evaluate how time is used in school. She encouraged us to picture a target, with the outermost ring being "allocated school time." This represents all of the time students spend in school. The next ring going toward the center is "allocated classroom time," or time students physically spend in the classroom. This is followed by "instructional time" (which excludes class time spent in noninstructional activities), and at the center of the target is "academic learning time." Silva defined this last category as "the time in which students are actually engaged in learning." With each successive layer, the amount of time spent gets smaller, so that when we reach the center, academic learning time, very little time remains. To no one's surprise, Silva's literature review suggests that increases in time dedicated to the outermost rings—allocated school time or class time—have less effect on student learning than increases of time to the innermost rings—instructional or academic learning time.

However, even without complex measurement of student engagement, school leaders we work with find it eye-opening to document the planned use of time. We use a framework that quantifies a more detailed set of time categories for how schools might use allotted time or "student time at school" (Shields & Miles, 2008):

- **Student time at school.** The number of hours between arrival and dismissal each day.
- **Instructional time.** The total number of hours of instruction.
- **Core academic time.** Time in English, math, science, social studies, and foreign language courses.
- **Noncore academic time.** Time in all other academic courses, including physical education.
- **Support and enrichment time.** Supervised study time, tutorial time, advisory periods, or other enrichment activities such as internships.
- **Maintenance and unassigned time.** Passing periods, lunch, and free periods, including study halls in which students are not directly supervised by certified instructors.
- **Release time.** Time that students are excused from attending school either for work, because they are ahead on graduation requirements, or for some other reason.

Before we dive into a discussion on maximizing time on academic subjects, we wish to clarify that we are not implying that schools should eliminate art, music, or other noncore academic subjects from the curriculum. Many high-performing schools we have studied enjoy rich and vibrant arts, music, and foreign language programs even though they require many of their students to spend significantly more time each day in core academic subjects (especially literacy and math). Instead, we encourage schools to *organize* their time in ways that allow all students to spend the appropriate amount of time in literacy and math for the level of their progress while also offering a rich and diverse curriculum that addresses their students' needs.

Figure 5.1 illustrates how a typical school might organize its use of time by these activities. Note that these figures do not come from a random sample of schools and so have no particular claim to being an "average" value, but instead are our attempt to typify what we have seen in dozens of districts.

Figure 5.1   Typical school: Minutes per key activity by school type

Time	Elementary School	Middle School	High School	Average
Time at school	6.4 hours	6.4 hours	6.6 hours	6.5 hours
Instructional time	4.9 hours	4.6 hours	4.60 hours	4.7 hours
• Core academics	3.6 hours	3.1 hours	2.75 hours	3.3 hours
• Noncore classes	1.3 hours	1.5 hours	1.85 hours	1.4 hours
Support and enrichment	0.3 hours	0.4 hours	0.5 hours	0.4 hours
Maintenance	1.2 hours	1.4 hours	1.5 hours	1.3 hours
Release time	0	Varies	Varies	N/A

NOTE: Maintenance time in this example includes a lunch (30 minutes in elementary and 45 minutes in secondary schools), five 6-minute passing periods (secondary), a 30-minute recess (elementary), and a 12-minute homeroom period (both) for announcements, attendance, and other administrative activities. Support and enrichment, at the elementary level, includes tutoring and other enrichment activities. At most secondary schools, many students have internships or supervised study time. Schools that have a schoolwide advisory period would have a much larger block for support and enrichment.

These figures may be easier to interpret as percentages of the amount of time students spend at school. Figure 5.2 presents the same information as percentages.

Notice that schools (at all levels) typically spend 75% or less of their time at school on instruction and secondary schools spend less than 50% of time on core academics in secondary settings. Organizing time in this way is a choice, not an imperative.

Figure 5.2   Typical school: Student activities as percentage of time at school

Time	Elementary School	Middle School	High School	Average
Time at school	100%	100%	100%	100%
Instructional time	76%	71%	66%	73%
• Core academics	56%	48%	42%	49%
• Noncore classes	20%	23%	24%	22%
Support and enrichment	5%	6%	11%	7%
Maintenance	19%	22%	23%	21%
Release time	0	Varies	Varies	N/A

Maximizing Time Principle H: Maximizing Time, Including Longer Blocks of Uninterrupted Time, That Students Spend on Academic Subjects

High-performing schools strategically maximize their total time on academic subjects and include longer blocks of uninterrupted time. To accomplish these goals, they might vary the lengths of classes for different subjects, stagger start times for different cohorts of students (and teachers), adopt block schedules, rotate bell schedules across multiple days and weeks, or invest more time and attention in extracurricular activities. Some high-performing schools add significant time to the school day (Shields & Miles, 2008), but they consistently work hard to make the best use of the time they have (Jenkins, Queen, & Algozzine, 2002). Figure 5.3 compares the way time is used in typical schools with what we see in strategic schools.

The factors listed in Figure 5.3 work together to minimize instructional time in typical schools. Consider an example of a typical high school, in which the attendance rate hovers around 80%, with these time use problems. As Figure 5.4 shows, fourteen minutes of received instruction per day per subject equates to an average of one hour and 10 minutes of actual instruction each day in the combined subjects of English, math, science, social studies, and foreign languages for four years of high school.

Block Scheduling as a Way to Maximize Time and Minimize Interruptions

Block scheduling is such an important scheduling policy option that it deserves special mention here. The term *block scheduling* refers to creating longer blocks of time (e.g., double periods) that may meet for only one semester or for fewer sessions per week. This strategy enables teachers to use time more flexibly and to engage in learning activities, such as science labs, that may take more time than the standard 50-minute period. Having fewer periods per day also increases total instructional time because it reduces "passing time," the time students spend moving between one class and the next.

To date, research on block scheduling does not show consistent results. Some studies find a positive effect of block scheduling (Deuel & Stoyco, 1999; Trenta & Newman, 2002; Weller & McLeskey, 2000), whereas other studies note either no effect or a negative academic effect of block scheduling (Gruber & Onwuegbuzie, 2001; Jenkins et al., 2002; Lawrence & McPherson, 2002; Rice, Croninger, & Roellke, 2002). In an analysis of 58 empirical studies of block scheduling in high schools, Zapeda and Mayers (2001) concluded that block scheduling

Figure 5.3 Maximizing time for academics in typical versus strategic schools

Practice	Typical School	Strategic School
Schedule is chosen based on assessment of student needs.	Schedule is adopted for ease of implementation and applies to all students equally regardless of how far behind they are in core subjects.	School leadership team recrafts the schedule, sometimes annually, to match time allocation with needs of students—subgroups and individuals.
Schedule meets needs of teachers in school context.	Schedule is constrained by same union contract and district policies that apply to all district schools.	Schedule may differ from other schools to increase planning time or professional development opportunities, or meet other teacher priorities.
Schedule maximizes time on highest-priority subjects.	Less than 50% of time is spent on core academics in secondary schools (60% in elementary schools); time allotted equally by subject in secondary schools with approximately 35% spent on English/ language arts (ELA) and math.	Students who struggle are given sufficient opportunity to catch up with peers in core academic subjects, focusing on ELA and math.
Careful consideration is given to amount of instructional time.	Maintenance time not considered when choosing bell schedule.	Schedule crafted to maximize percentage of day spent on instruction or support and enrichment activities.
There is accountability for use of instructional time.	Teachers have freedom to use classroom time as they choose with little direction or accountability; PA announcements and other problems may cut instruction time in half (National Education Commission on Time and Learning, 1994; Smith, 1998).	Teachers have clear expectations for how to use instruction time and are held accountable for spending sufficient time in English and math (at elementary level) and making good use of time; administrators avoid interrupting instruction.

Figure 5.4   The math of typical students' instructional time per subject
per day

Student Day	300 Minutes
60% of student day is in core academics	180 minutes/day in core academics
Divided by five core academic subjects (math, English, social studies, science, and foreign language)	36 minutes/subject/day
Subtract frequent interruptions, which cut instructional time in half	18 minutes/subject/day
Subtract time missed because students attend school only 80% of the year	14 minutes/subject/day

seemed to increase student grade point averages and improve school climate, but its effects on teacher practices, student achievement, and attendance were inconsistent. A possible reconciliation of these seemingly contradictory findings is that block schedules may be ineffective unless accompanied by support and professional development that help teachers make effective use of longer time periods (Marchant & Paulson, 2001; Veal & Flinders, 2001; Zapeda & Mayers, 2001). As with other strategies, schedules must be aligned with instructional purpose and student need.

Case Examples of Maximizing Academic Time

Case 1—Rafael Hernandez Elementary School, Boston. Long literacy blocks have become common in elementary schools. National models such as Success for All and America's Choice are built around literacy blocks, but most homegrown schedules also incorporate no less than 90 minutes of literacy every day. To illustrate how a literacy block works, we have chosen to use the example of the Rafael Hernandez elementary school in Boston (see Figure 5.5). Hernandez is a PreK–8 Spanish-bilingual school. On most mornings, excluding Tuesdays, the school organizes a 100-minute literacy block from 9:20 a.m. to 11 a.m. On Tuesdays, the literacy block is only 50 minutes, and a subject specialist teaches the class to provide planning time for teachers.

The schedule creates long literacy blocks and collaboration time. The school also organizes to bring trained instructors into the class during literacy so that they can create very small literacy groups of 5 to 6 students in kindergarten through third grade and 10 to 12 students in Grades 5 to 8.

Figure 5.5   The Rafael Hernandez Master Schedule

Time	Monday	Tuesday	Wednesday	Thursday	Friday
9:10–9:20	Before-school work				
9:20–10:15	Reading	Computers	Reading	Reading	Reading
10:15–11:00		Art			
11:00–11:50	Writer's Workshop	Reading	Writer's Workshop	Writer's Workshop	Writer's Workshop
11:50–12:10	Skills math	Math	Math	Math	Math
12:10–2:50	Lunch and recess				
12:50–1:45	Math	Math	Math	Math	Math
1:45–2:30	Music	Expeditionary Learning	Expeditionary Learning	Expeditionary Learning	Expeditionary Learning
2:30–3:15	Gym				
3:15–3:25	Dismissal	Dismissal	Dismissal	Dismissal	Dismissal

SOURCE: From *Five Case Studies on Revising School Schedules*, by R. Shields, 1999, Alexandria, VA: New American Schools. Reprinted with permission.

The combination of long literacy blocks, flexible grouping, and individual attention helped propel Hernandez to a much-improved level of student performance. The school faculty and leadership review and adapt the schedule every year to continue learning from their collective experience (Shields, 1999).

Case 2—Perspectives Charter School, Chicago. The example of Perspectives Charter School in Chicago is also illustrative. Note that our inclusion of a charter school here is deliberate. Although we have studied many schools that have transformed their bell schedules in the context of public school systems, in recent years, increasing numbers of reform-minded school leaders are opening charter schools to facilitate the radical redesign of their schools, including flexible block schedules and other innovative scheduling options.

Perspectives Charter School serves more than 300 students in Grades 6 through 12. It aims to help students develop character and prepare for college. To graduate prepared for college, Perspectives' students are required to spend a great deal of instructional time on core academics: four years of English, math, science, social studies, and DEAR (Drop Everything and Read; see Figure 5.6). To work on character development, they also spend a great deal of time in support and enrichment activities (in this case, the Disciplined Life advisory program). These two focuses leave comparatively little time for noncore academic subjects such as drama, art, health, and music.

To spend so much time in core academics and retain a robust support and enrichment program, Perspectives needed a new schedule. The first step was to lengthen the school day. Given the notoriously short 300 to 315 minutes of other Chicago public schools, this was a vital step for this school. They added 80 minutes per day (the Chicago equivalent of nine school weeks) to the calendar. High school students at Perspectives attend school from 8:30 a.m. until 3:30 p.m. on Mondays, Tuesdays, Thursdays, Fridays, and every other Wednesday. On the opposite Wednesdays, students are dismissed at 1 p.m., making the average length of the school day 395 minutes. They also organized the schedule into double blocks to honor a commitment to experiential learning.

As a result of these scheduling changes and the high graduation requirements, Perspectives students spend 67% of the day in core academic classes and a whopping 27% in English/language arts (ELA), which is a critical focus for these students. Combined with the longer day, Figure 5.7 shows that this time allocation results in much more time in core subjects than the average Chicago public high school student receives (Shields & Miles, 2008).

How does the schedule work? The student schedule is organized so that in classes such as English, history, science, and art, students have a 50-minute period two days per week and a double block of 102 minutes once a week to allow for longer blocks of uninterrupted learning time and

Figure 5.6 Perspectives Charter School graduation requirements

4 years of English, math, science, social studies	4 years of DEAR
2 years of Spanish	4 years of "A Disciplined Life"
2 semester internships	2 semesters of art
1 social justice class	1 semester of drama
2 college preparation classes	2 semesters of health

NOTE: DEAR = Drop Everything and Read.

Figure 5.7   Perspectives Charter School: Minutes per day by subject

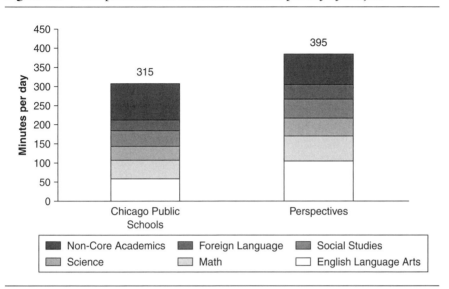

project-based learning. Meanwhile, other classes, such as math and Spanish, meet every day (with the exception of Wednesday) as the daily repetition of this material is viewed as more important than fewer periods of longer blocks of time. Every other Wednesday is spent in Field Studies, in which teachers extend classroom studies by developing units to explore in locations throughout Chicago. Teachers accompany students on these field studies. As a result, the typical student schedule looks something like Figure 5.8 (Shields & Miles, 2008).

Case Example 3—Harrison Place High School. Harrison Place High School (Grades 9–12, enrollment 1,550) is another inspirational school that crafted a custom schedule to meet its needs (Archibald, 2001). Located in a large urban district in the Midwestern United States, the school was closed in 1989 due to perennial poor academic performance. It was later reopened as five distinct learning communities. Its underlying population didn't change. Fifteen percent of students were on individualized education plans, 85% were African American, about 15% were white, and half of the students qualified for free or reduced-price lunch. By 2001, Harrison had transformed from the lowest to the highest performance category in its district (based on annual yearly progress and overall student performance).

The student schedule, a flexible block schedule, was a key centerpiece of the successful transformation of this school. Before Harrison moved to flexible block scheduling, the student schedule featured seven 49-minute

Figure 5.8   Perspectives Charter School typical student schedule

Time	Monday	Tuesday	Wednesday (A week)	Wednesday (B week)	Thursday	Friday
8:30–9:00	DEAR	DEAR	DEAR	DEAR	DEAR	DEAR
9:00–9:50	Spanish	Elective		Social Justice/ Internship/ College Preparation	Math	Spanish
9:52–10:42	Science	Elective			Spanish	Science
10:44–11:34	Math	Math			English	Math
11:36–12:26	History	Spanish	Field Studies	Early dismissal for students (professional development for teachers)	English	History
12:28–1:06	Lunch	Lunch			Lunch	Lunch
1:08–1:48	ADL	ADL			ADL	ADL
1:50–2:40	Elective	History			Science	Elective
2:42–3:32	English	History			Science	English

NOTE: DEAR = Drop Everything and Read; ADL = A Disciplined Life.

class periods and a 30-minute lunch period each day. At any given time, students were enrolled in English, math, science, social studies, a special program class, and two additional classes, from the choices of foreign language (which we count as a core academic course), physical education, music, or art. This schedule resulted in students spending either 196 or 245 minutes in core academic courses, 58% or 70% of their time at school, depending on the nature of their electives and special program class. The prereform and postreform student schedules are listed in Figures 5.9 and 5.10.

Under the flexible block schedule implemented in 1999–2000, there were eight 45-minute class periods, or bells, plus a 30-minute lunch period. But three of these 45-minute class periods were combined to make one 135-minute academic block of English and social studies. Three more were combined for a math and science block of the same duration.

Importantly, the schedule allowed students to focus more time on core academics without losing the ability to have a rich offering of elective

Figure 5.9   Harrison Place High School's prereform student schedule (1998–1999)

8:00–8:20	Student arrival	
8:20–8:30	Locker period	
8:30–9:19	Bell 1	
9:23–10:12	Bell 2	
10:16–11:05	Bell 3	
Lunch A	**Lunch B**	**Lunch C**
Lunch 11:09–11:39 Bell 4 11:43–12:32 Bell 5 12:36–1:25	Bell 4 11:09–11:58 Lunch 12:02–12:32 Bell 5 12:36–1:25	Bell 4 11:09–11:58 Bell 5 12:02–12:51 Lunch 12:55–1:25
1:29–2:18	Bell 6	
2:22–3:11	Bell 7	
3:11–3:20	Dismissal	

SOURCE: From *A Case Study of Dramatic Resource Reallocation to Improve Student Achievement: Harrison Place High School*, by S. Archibald, 2001, Madison, WI: Consortium for Policy Research in Education Working Paper, University of Wisconsin–Madison. Reprinted with permission.

classes. Students still had the opportunity to take two special courses, such as foreign language and art, for 45 minutes each. Under this new flexible block schedule, Harrison students now spent between 292.5 minutes and 315 minutes in the core academic subjects of English, math, science, social studies, and foreign languages.

In percentage terms, this means that 67% to 90% of the student day was dedicated to core academics in 2000–2001. The increase of 70 minutes or more of core academic instructional time was accomplished while adding only 19 extra minutes to the school day.

The change to block scheduling had some ancillary effects that were considered positive:

- The number of distinct classes taught by teachers (preps) decreased.
- The student count (teacher load) of core academic teachers dropped to twice a class size.
- Teachers had more control of how to allocate time in the 135-minute blocks and were better able to conduct labs or other experiential learning activities.

Figure 5.10   Harrison Place High School's flexible block schedule (1999–2001)

8:00–8:20	Student arrival	
8:20–8:30	Locker period	
8:30–9:15	Bell 1[a]	
9:19–10:04	Bell 2	
10:08–10:53	Bell 3	
Lunch A	**Lunch B**	**Lunch C**
Lunch 10:57–11:27 Bell 4 11:31–12:15 Bell 5 12:19–1:03	Bell 4 10:57–11:47 Lunch 11:45–12:15 Bell 5 12:19–1:03	Bell 4 10:57–11:47 Bell 5 11:45–12:29 Lunch 12:33–1:03
1:07–1:52	Bell 6[b]	
1:56–2:41	Bell 7	
2:45–3:30	Bell 8	
3:30–3:40	Dismissal	

a. Periods 1–3 = 135-minute academic block.

b. Periods 6–8 = 135-minute academic block.

SOURCE: From *A Case Study of Dramatic Resource Reallocation to Improve Student Achievement: Harrison Place High School*, by S. Archibald, 2001, Madison, WI: Consortium for Policy Research in Education Working Paper, University of Wisconsin–Madison. Reprinted with permission.

Maximizing Academic Time Principle I: Varying Time and Instructional Programs to Ensure All Students Meet Rigorous Academic Standards

Research shows that extending the right kind of time to the students who need it most can improve students' learning and effectively close achievement gaps between poor and minority students and their more affluent peers. It can also enhance the rigor and relevance of a school's curriculum by providing more time for core academic subjects without sacrificing other subjects. And it can improve teaching by providing opportunities for teacher planning, collaboration and professional development. (Silva, 2007, p. 16)

Students have different needs. Even demographically similar students bring varied backgrounds and different learning styles to the learning process. Yet most schools provide support and intervention based primarily on broad categorical or programmatic distinctions, not on the specific content skills that students need to master. English-language learners may be treated one way, with a certain set of interventions. Students with special needs will have a different set of interventions, determined largely by the level and restrictiveness of earmarked "categorical" special-education funds (or staff) the school receives. Some schools see the goal of providing extra support to be remediation. We prefer the concept of "accelerated learning" coined by economist Henry Levin (1991). Accelerated learning means helping struggling students—some of whom may be years behind their age peers—rapidly catch up academically so that they can rejoin their peers. Many types of categorical support provided by schools (i.e., teaching assistants, program coordinators, or the pull-out programs described in earlier chapters) do not actually increase the amount of time these students spend in core academic subjects.

When extra time is given, it often comes at times or in ways that are not optimal for accelerating learning. Specifically, most extra time is provided during summer school, during afterschool programs, or in the form of repeated classes. Often, summer school and afterschool teachers do not know what each student is learning (or not learning) in his or her regular education program. This can render the extra time ineffective or inefficient. Similarly, requiring students to repeat failed courses year after year almost guarantees that struggling students will not catch up, and it certainly ensures boredom. We note that there are effective summer school and afterschool programs. Our point is that these programs by their nature have special challenges that must be addressed to be effective.

The example of a northeastern district we studied illustrates this last point. On paper, it looked like many of this district's students were being required to take four years of math. But on closer inspection, 40% of twelfth-grade students were still taking Algebra I, some for the third or fourth time.

The strategic schools we studied did not rely on broad categorical distinctions to identify the needs of students. Instead, they assessed student skill levels and learning styles. Then they adjusted the instructional program (including time on task) accordingly. As the strategies for doing this differ between the elementary and secondary levels, we turn to these separately.

How Strategic Elementary Schools Vary Time on Task

Because homeroom teachers remain with one classroom of children all day long, they usually do this by grouping and regrouping their students flexibly throughout the day. Among other things, this can allow each student to work on some subjects more than others, as needed. There are several strategies for supporting this type of instructional flexibility, including tutoring, small-group support teachers, and other examples we discussed in the previous chapter. We will not rehash those ideas here. We would, however, remind the reader of the case of the Children's School of Rochester (CSR). CSR maximized its ability to organize flexible groups by combining all grade-level classes into family groups. Each family group's collaborative team of three or more teachers collaborated daily to determine both how to group students and how much time each group of students should spend on a particular lesson. By mixing and remixing small groups and desk work throughout the day, it was possible for some students to spend far more time on math than other students.

How Strategic Secondary Schools Vary Time on Task

Consider the example of Tech Boston Academy (TBA). TBA is a "pilot" school in Boston, Massachusetts, that serves Grades 9 through 12. Pilot schools receive significant flexibility from union work rules and district curriculum requirements. TBA aims to prepare its students for careers in technology, computer science, and engineering while also preparing them for college. Part of their explicit instructional strategy is to individualize students' schedules based on personal need.

TBA achieves this customization first by extending the school day, giving students an average of 7.5 hours per day in school, which is 90 minutes longer than students in traditional Boston Public Schools. Most days, students at TBA are in school from 8:00 a.m. to 3:00 p.m. On Monday, Tuesday, and Thursday, ninth- and tenth-grade students are required to stay for an extended period of test preparation and tutoring until 4:00 p.m. Students in the upper grades *earn* the right to leave at 3:00 p.m., but those students who are struggling academically or are not completing their homework are required to stay until 4:00 p.m. The TBA teacher contract states a commitment to be in school between 8:15 a.m. and 4:30 p.m. Monday through Thursday and 8:15 a.m. and 3:30 p.m. on Friday.

TBA also organizes a "Project Room" period to strategically target extra academic support to both low- and high-performing students in their regular school day (see Figure 5.11). Project Room gives teachers the opportunity to work either with small groups or individual students to help them access technology, complete homework, or work on areas of need. For most TBA students, 45 of the 90 extra school minutes are spent in Project Room. This investment in individually targeted support is substantial. On average, TBA students receive the equivalent of 26 more days of support and enrichment than students in other Boston Public Schools (Shields & Miles, 2008).

Figure 5.11   Ninth-grade sample Tech Boston Academy student schedule

Period	Monday	Tuesday	Wednesday	Thursday	Friday
1	Homeroom	Homeroom	Homeroom	Homeroom	Homeroom
2	Digital Art	IT Essentials	Freshman Seminar	Learning Center	Web Development
3	World History	Physics	ELA	Algebra	World History
4	Algebra	World History	Physics	ELA	Algebra
5	Project Room	Project Room	Project Room	Project Room	Project Room
6	ELA	Algebra	World History	Physics	ELA
7	Physics	ELA	Algebra	World History	Physics
8	Support and Enrichment	Support and Enrichment		Support and Enrichment	

NOTE: ELA = English/language arts.

TBA crafts each student's schedule by looking at many data points. Principal Mary Skipper explains, "My goal is to constantly maximize the amount of instructional time, and we are able to build in student support during the school day. We make curriculum and scheduling choices based on student need." For example, if students get identified through their Massachusetts Comprehensive Assessment System profile as needing math enrichment, ELA enrichment, or tutoring, they get placed in that course instead of Project Room. But TBA does not stop there. Teachers assess students at various points in the year to identify strengths and weaknesses and provide immediate extra support (Shields & Miles, 2008). This strategy requires considerable investment of teacher time to ensure that the more-flexible blocks of time are used effectively. We return to scheduling issues in Chapter 10 when we present ideas on how to craft a schedule that aligns with a school's talents, needs, priorities, and instructional approach.

PART III

How to Make the Most of Your School's People, Time, and Money

What is a strategic school? When we call a school strategic, we mean that it has allocated all of its resources to support a schoolwide, instructionally-based vision. We started this book by describing how the typical organizational structures in education—classrooms divided by grade and subject, seven-hour days cut into short periods, and teachers who work independently—do not always effectively support the instructional design of a school. Legacy structures make it difficult to organize resources in strategic ways, even when school leaders have a clear instructional vision. Strategic school leaders must also have the ability and will to re-examine these typical structures and rethink them when they don't fit school needs.

Put differently, every school already has an "organizational design," but not every school has a strategic organizational design that links its resources with its instructional priorities, its overriding purpose. By *organizational design*, we mean something different than instructional design—although the two intertwine. Instructional design refers to the choice and definition of curriculum goals and content, instructional materials, and assessment practices. These instructional design decisions also include whether curriculum material will be interdisciplinary or thematic. For example, interdisciplinary models might combine subjects such as English and social studies into one integrated set of units, or they might weave a common set of skills such as writing and numeracy deliberately through all subject areas. A thematic approach might explore selected ideas or disciplines across all subjects wherever possible, such as social justice or a particular approach to problem solving.

A school's instructional design informs its organizational design—but it isn't the same thing. For instance, consider two schools that decide to have a humanities focus. They adopt the same curriculum and instructional pedagogy. However, one school combines English and social studies instruction into one class, while the other does not. One school adopts a four-by-four schedule, while the other does not. Although the schools have a similar instructional approach, they have very different organizational designs. Some organizational design decisions flow automatically from instructional design choices, while others are independent. The goal of the planning process in strategic schools is to create an organizational design that supports an instructional design.

The following section of this book, Part III, is an implementation section. It walks through the creation of four components of a strategic organizational design:

Four Components of a Strategic School Plan

1. **A strategic plan to assign teachers and group students** that defines how teachers will be grouped with students for instruction throughout the day

2. **A master schedule** that prescribes the amount and allocation of student and teacher time

3. **A human capital strategy** that describes the comprehensive set of recruiting, hiring, and professional development strategies the school will use to build a community of highly-skilled professionals

4. **An implementation and staffing plan** that defines how each staff member, including those in nonteaching positions, works in support of student learning

How to Use This Section

We recommend that all readers start this section by reading Chapter 6. Chapter 6 presents the case of the Fleming school, which is used in each implementation chapter. It also discusses the first two steps of the strategic planning process and contains information that will enable readers to complete the other chapters. After completing Chapter 6, readers can freely move through Chapters 7 to 9 in any order they wish. These chapters cover the first three components of a strategic organizational design. After that, readers can move to Chapter 10, Putting It All Together, and to the conclusion.

We invite all readers to download blank copies of the tools and templates presented from www.educationresourcestrategies.org and to create a strategic plan for their own school as they work through each chapter and follow the case of the Fleming School.

Chapter 6: Introduction to the Fleming Case and to strategic planning and assessment tools

Chapter 7: How to create a staffing and grouping plan

Chapter 8: How to create a strategic master schedule

Chapter 9: How to create a strategic plan to continuously improve teaching quality

Chapter 10: Putting It All Together

Chapter 11: Conclusion

The Six Steps of the Planning Process in Strategic Schools

As school leaders create each of the components of a strategic plan, they follow a similar planning process. This process forms the outline of Chapters 7 to 9:

1. Determine your school's highest-priority academic needs.

2. Assess how well your resource organizations meet your academic needs.

3. Set concrete goals to meet your highest-priority needs.

4. Identify and evaluate options for accomplishing your goals.

5. Create a strategy by choosing a set of options that works in your school's context.

6. Decide on ways to measure progress toward your goals and then measure them. (We discuss Step 6 in Chapter 10, "Putting It All Together.")

Tools for Strategic Schools

6

*How Well Does Your School Use
People, Time, and Money?*

In this chapter, we begin the first two steps of the strategic planning process:

- Assessing the academic needs and priorities of a school's students and faculty
- Determining whether the current organizational design is allocating people, time, and money to effectively address those needs

To make this discussion more concrete, we will conduct it in the context of a case study, the Fleming School, which we will follow until the book's conclusion.

This chapter introduces the case of the Fleming School and presents a brief assessment of the academic needs of Fleming's students and teachers. It also contains a series of tools that will help readers make strategic plans for their own school as they complete the exercises in Chapters 7 to 9 for the Fleming School. The tools include

1. The Elementary Resource Measurement Worksheet, which suggests specific metrics and calculations you can perform on elementary schools to better understand resource use

2. The Secondary Resource Measurement Worksheet, which suggests specific metrics and calculations you can perform on secondary schools to better understand resource use

3. The Strategic School Resource Diagnostic Tool, which asks a series of questions about how your school uses resources

4. The Fleming Teacher Inventory

Blank copies of these worksheets can be downloaded free at www.education resourcestrategies.org.

INTRODUCTION TO THE FLEMING SCHOOL

The Fleming School is an actual school that we have partnered with. Only the name has been disguised. The school serves 752 students in Grades K through 8. Of students, 93% qualify for free or reduced-price lunch, 31% are English language learners, and 20% are special-education students. The student demographics are as follows: 62% Hispanic, 29% African American, 8% white, and 1% other. The school recently learned that it did not meet adequate yearly progress (AYP).

There is not much of a collaborative culture in the building. Most teachers view meetings and visits to other teachers' classrooms as a waste of time. They would prefer using this time to "do their own work." In addition, the bilingual teachers and the regular-education teachers operate as two distinct groups. When they do participate in collaborative planning or other professional development, they tend to cluster in bilingual/ monolingual groups, as opposed to grade-level groups.

Fleming School leaders are working with the central office to meet AYP. Together, they hope to accomplish the following strategic planning tasks:

*   Assess the academic needs of Fleming's students and teachers.
*   Reassign staff and regroup students in ways that focus time and effort on the school's highest-priority goals in ways most likely to improve student performance.
*   Adopt a new master schedule that allocates student and teacher time to the school's priorities in ways that support other elements of the strategic plan, such as professional development and staffing and grouping strategies.
*   Create a strategic plan for improving the quality of teaching.
*   Review each element of the overall strategic plan for fit and then implement the plan.

Step 1: What Are the Most Pressing Academic Needs of Fleming Students?

The Fleming School has serious performance challenges. No Fleming students score at the advanced levels of the state test, and less than a quarter of students score proficient on either the English/language arts (ELA) or math components (see Figures 6.1 and 6.2). Performance scores decline from elementary to middle grades.

The problems in math are significantly worse than in ELA. Nearly half of all students score in the lowest math category. By Grade 8, a full 63% of students have fallen to this category.

A quick scan of Fleming's disaggregated data shows that African American and Hispanic students score similarly to each other at all grade levels, in all subjects. There are too few students of other races to note any comparative significance in their scores. Girls slightly outperform boys in ELA; girls' and boys' scores are similar in math. Almost all Fleming students qualify for free and reduced-price lunch, so desegregating based on socioeconomic status isn't relevant. However, there are predictable gaps in performance among students in regular education, special education, and ELL.

Figure 6.1 Fleming overall English/language arts state results

Grade	Percentage Advanced	Percentage Proficient	Percentage Needs Improvement	Percentage Warning
Grade 4	0%	22%	42%	36%
Grade 7	0%	26%	39%	35%

Figure 6.2 Fleming overall math state results

Grade	Percentage Advanced	Percentage Proficient	Percentage Needs Improvement	Percentage Warning
Grade 4	0%	11%	38%	51%
Grade 6	0%	20%	37%	43%
Grade 8	0%	6%	31%	63%

A more detailed item analysis of the Fleming state test scores high-lights some important content-related patterns at all grade levels that reflect trouble with thinking critically and solving problems:

- Fleming students score poorly on open-response questions.
- In math, students have particular trouble with multistep problems.
- In literacy, students have particular trouble with questions requiring inference and with questions about nonfiction texts.

It is also important to note that student performance varies significantly within grades by individual teacher, with only the first-grade teachers having consistently strong student performance results in both ELA and math. This suggests that we should also look at the needs of Fleming teachers.

To summarize, it appears that the most pressing academic problems of Fleming students are

- Math scores start low and decline as students progress.
- Critical thinking and problem solving are weak across the curriculum.
- ELA student performance does not meet school goals.

Step 2: Does Fleming Devote Its People, Time, and Money to Its Highest-Priority Needs?

Having now identified the priority needs of students and teachers, we can begin the second step of the strategic planning process: determining whether Fleming's current resource use matches its highest-priority needs. In the chapters that follow, we will examine resource use at Fleming as it relates to the specific task of that chapter. Here, we present a set of tools that helps us (a) measure *how* resources are organized, (b) evaluate how *well* resources are organized (in relation to the principles introduced in earlier chapters), and (c) create a simple inventory of how talent and experience are distributed across the school's organization.

Three tools help us accomplish these tasks:

- Resource Measurement Worksheet
- Strategic School Resource Diagnostic Tool
- Inventory of Teacher Skills

Resource Measurement Worksheet

This worksheet (Figures 6.3 and 6.4, for elementary and secondary schools) helps school leaders describe *how* they use their people, time, and money. It asks school leaders to complete a brief series of calculations that help quantify the school's use of resources. The result is a series of metrics and indicators that we find useful for evaluating resource use and comparing investment levels across different programs and interventions. Our experience suggests this is rarely done systematically in most schools. We have created separate formats for elementary and secondary schools. This is because the indicators differ slightly by school level. The answers from this worksheet flow into the Strategic School Resource Diagnostic Tool, which offers suggestions for interpreting your answers.

Strategic School Resource Diagnostic Tool

This tool (Figure 6.5) helps school leaders evaluate how well they use their people, time, and money in relation to the guiding resource principles discussed in Part II. Along the left side of the tool, we present the nine resource principles in order, grouped by the three overarching resource strategies: teaching quality, individual attention, and time on core academics. In the center column, we present a set of questions to consider as well as some things to look for (we call them leading indicators) to determine whether your school is strategically adhering to each principle. We look at class sizes, teacher and student time, and professional development in a variety of nuanced ways. On the right of the chart, we give hints and tips for interpreting the data and for identifying issues that may need additional investigation. Note that to complete this review, it is helpful to first complete the Resource Measurement Worksheet.

Inventory of Teacher Skills (Fleming School Sample)

The final tool presented in this chapter is the Inventory of Teacher Skills to help school leaders evaluate the skills, experience, training, and performance of individual teachers and of the faculty as a whole (see Figure 6.6 for the Fleming Teacher Inventory). The Inventory of Teacher Skills is a tool to help school leaders systematically adjust assignments and responsibilities to match changing situations. Most school leaders we know keep a mental inventory of teachers' experience, training, and certification, and they have a good sense of the interests and energy of individual teachers. But when leaders don't organize this knowledge in any formal way, the information can be lost. The inventory presented here is more deliberate. On the other hand, it is not set in stone. Any useful inventory must be specific to the school's instructional design and able to evolve over time. At a minimum, the inventory should include details of the faculty's education, skills, experience, certification credentials, and team leader status. It should also include some sort of overall evaluation, even if only a subjective rating of quality on a four-star scale based on the principal's judgment.

The sample inventory we provide here has been designed specifically for the Fleming school and so contains additional columns useful to the Fleming school's situation. Specifically, it captures whether teachers have received training on two key initiatives in English and math. It also captures the principal's own subjective judgment of how well teachers are implementing each of these new initiatives. We will discuss the implications of the Fleming Teacher Inventory when we discuss the design of a strategic professional development plan.

How to Use These Tools in Your Own School

In the chapters that follow, readers will refer to these tools frequently to gain a deeper understanding of the Fleming case example. We also encourage school leaders to download blank copies of each form and fill them out for their own school as part of their overall strategic planning process. How might this work? We recommend that a small school leadership team complete these tools together, perhaps as part of the school planning cycle over a three-month period. To complete this diagnostic exercise, make sure you have the following materials on hand:

- List of student enrollment by grade and program (special education, bilingual, etc.)
- List of entire staff (including those funded through Title I and other external grants)
- Copy of the master schedule (grade and subject or activity each teacher is working with and when. Include lunch duty, planning time, etc.)
- Copy of your school's Comprehensive School Plan
- Copy of your school's budget
- Calculator

After completing the three tools included here, you should have a deeper understanding of how your school is using resources, including teacher talent, and how well that stacks up against the resource principles in this book. This diagnostic knowledge is essential to creating a strategic school. As we have discussed before, it is essential that leaders not try to address all of their school's challenges at the same time. Instead, leaders should ask, "Given my context, what changes would have the most immediate impact?"

The following chapters provide concrete suggestions for addressing some of the most common resource challenges. We do not expect all readers to dive deeply into every chapter. Instead, we hope you will use the findings from your own needs assessment to guide you so that you delve most deeply into the implementation chapters that address your highest priorities.

That said, although it is important to be strategic, it is also true that teaching quality is the single most important piece of a successful resource strategy. If you find that you are low in this area (Strategy 1), then this is probably the area to tackle first by designing a strategic professional development plan (in Chapter 9). If you find that you are low in all areas, you should also start with teaching quality. You will quickly find that tackling teaching quality has implications for the scheduling and budget, because you will need to find common planning time and resources for expert support.

The worksheets follow. They are also available for free download at www.educationresourcestrategies.org.

Figure 6.3   Resource measurement worksheet: Elementary grades

Directions: Complete the following Resource Measurement Worksheet to quantify your school's use of resources. You will use these calculations to complete the Strategic School Resource Diagnostic Tool in Figure 6.5.	
For Grades K–6	*School Calculations*
A. Student Enrollment These entries should add up to your school's total enrollment. For example, even though special-education resource students participate in the regular-education program, count them here in the special-education resource line. "Self-contained" refers to students who are assigned to a homeroom or home base class that remains together for most or all of the school day.	Regular Education _____ Special-Education Resource _____ ELL Self-Contained _____ Special-Education Self-Contained _____ Gifted Self-Contained _____ Total _____
B. Teaching Staff "Resource" teachers refers to teachers who work with students for part of the day to support special learning needs. These teachers do not have their own classroom. The most common of these are special-education resource teachers. You may have other resource teachers such as a reading resource, ELL, or gifted-education teachers. Create your own separate line, or code these as "other resource." Subject specialists are teachers who teach students from more than one class in a particular subject area such as art, music, physical education (PE), and computer skills. Some schools might use a librarian to teach some periods during the day—if so, that portion of time should be included in the subject specialist total. If an individual teaches only part of the day, then only that fraction of his or her time should be included in the total.	Regular-Education Classroom _____ Special-Education Resource _____ Other Resource _____ Subject Specialists _____ Special-Education Self-Contained _____ ELL Self-Contained _____ Other _____ Total _____
C. Overall School Average Students per Teacher (A divided by B) The number of students in all programs (total in A) divided by the number of teachers assigned to the school in all programs from B above. This includes classroom teachers, specialists, teachers paid for through Title I and other outside	

Figure 6.3 (Continued)

For Grades K–6	School Calculations
funding, and special-education teachers. It does not include pupil support professionals such as speech and other therapists, paraprofessionals, guidance counselors, and so on, unless they teach classes.	
D. Regular-Education Class Size Includes students who have special education needs who are served by resource teachers for part of the day but who are assigned to homeroom classes and spend much of their time there. It also includes ELL students if they are in regular classrooms and teachers paid for by Title I if they are used schoolwide as regular classroom teachers.	Average Range K _____ _____ 1 _____ _____ 2 _____ _____ 3 _____ _____ 4 _____ _____ 5 _____ _____ 6 _____ _____ Overall _____ _____
E. Percentage of Students Who Spend Most of Their Time in Regular-Education Classrooms Includes special-education students and English language learners who are assigned to a regular homeroom class but receive extra support from a resource teacher. In most schools, these are regular-education students, resource room, or ELL.	Average _____ Range _____
F. Percentage of Teachers Who Work With Students in Regular-Education Classrooms This includes regular-education classroom teachers and subject specialists such as art, music, and PE. It only includes special-education teachers if they work in inclusion settings that include regular-education program students.	
G. Special-Education Self-Contained Class Size This refers to students who are in classrooms most of the day with other students diagnosed with disabilities requiring special accommodations.	Average _____ Range _____

For Grades K–6	*School Calculations*
H. English Language Learner (ELL) Self-Contained Class Size This refers to students and teachers working in classes with only ELL students for most of the school day.	Average _____ Range _____
I. Gifted Self-Contained Class Size This refers to students in classrooms most of the day with other gifted students.	Average _____ Range _____
J. Size of Teacher-Facilitated Reading Groups (if applicable) This would apply if the school uses a strategy to create smaller reading groups during literacy periods by pushing staff into the classroom or by adding additional sections of skill-based instruction.	
K. Size of Teacher-Facilitated Math Groups (if applicable) This would apply if the school uses a strategy to create smaller groups during math periods by pushing staff into the classroom or by adding additional sections of skill-based instruction.	
L. Extra Instruction Time for Targeted Students (minutes per week) This refers to tutoring time, small-group academic attention, or afterschool or required help sessions.	• Maximum minutes of acceleration/week _____ • Maximum minutes of remediation/week _____
M. Student Minutes of . . . • **Literacy** (Fill out daily if your schedule is the same every day. If not, calculate weekly.) • **Math (weekly, daily)** • **Instruction** (Do not include lunch, homeroom, recess, or passing time in this number.) • **Total** (from start to dismissal)	Daily/Weekly — Percentage of Total Literature: _____ _____ Math: _____ _____ Instruction: _____ _____ Total: _____ 100%
N. Collaborative Planning Time Minutes per Week This number would not include instruction-free periods designated for individual planning, but only time that is scheduled and planned for strategically grouped teams of teachers to work together.	Regular Classroom Teachers _____ Special Subject Teachers _____

(Continued)

Figure 6.3 (Continued)

For Grades K–6	School Calculations		
O. Schoolwide Staff Development Days or Hours per Year This refers to time where all teachers have instruction-free time that is designated for professional development or planning purposes. This might include early release time (if not included above) and staff development days built into the teacher work calendar.			
Q. Teacher Experience: Percentage and number of teachers with three or fewer years of teaching experience.		Number	Percentage
	K	_____	_____
	1	_____	_____
	2	_____	_____
	3	_____	_____
	4	_____	_____
	5	_____	_____
	6	_____	_____
	Special Education	_____	_____
R. Percentage of Certified Teachers		Number	Percentage
	K	_____	_____
	1	_____	_____
	2	_____	_____
	3	_____	_____
	4	_____	_____
	5	_____	_____
	6	_____	_____
	Special Education	_____	_____
S. Teacher Salaries: Calculate the average teacher salary for the following:	Schoolwide Average Teacher Salary: _____ Average Homeroom Teacher Salary: _____ Average Special-Education Teacher Salary: _____ Average Bilingual Teacher Salary: _____ Average Specialist Salary: _____		

SOURCE: © Education Resource Strategies.

Figure 6.4 Resource measurement worksheet: Secondary grades

Directions: Complete the following Resource Measurement Worksheet to quantify your school's use of resources. You will use these calculations to complete the Strategic School Resource Diagnostic Tool in Figure 6.5. If the table cell is shaded, there is no need to calculate a number.

	Language Arts	Math	Social Studies	Science	Foreign Language	Physical Education	Other Elective	Overall School
A. Student Enrollment[1]								Reg Ed ⸺ Spec Ed Res ⸺ Spec Ed Self-Contained ⸺ ELL Self-Contained ⸺ Other ⸺ Total ⸺
B. Teaching Staff								Reg Ed ⸺ Spec Ed Res ⸺ Spec Ed Self-Contained ⸺ ELL Self-Contained ⸺ Other ⸺ Total ⸺
C. Overall School Average Students per Teacher[2]								

(Continued)

105

Figure 6.4 (Continued)

	Language Arts	Math	Social Studies	Science	Foreign Language	Physical Education	Other Elective	Overall School
D. Reg Ed Average Class Size[3]								
• Grade 6 or 9[4]	___						___	___
• Grade 7 or 10[4]	___						___	___
• Grade 8 or 11–12[4]	___						___	___
G. Spec Ed Self-Contained Average Class Size								
H. ELL Self-Contained Average Class Size								
I. Honors/Advanced Placement Average Class Size								
L. Extra Time for Targeted Students (min/week)[5]								
• Maximum minutes of acceleration/ week	___	___						___
• Maximum minutes of remediation/ week	___	___						

	Language Arts	Math	Social Studies	Science	Academic Elective	Nonacademic Elective	Non-instructional[7]	Overall School
M. Student Minutes per Week by Subject[6]								
• Grade 9	___	___	___	___	___	___	___	___
• Grade 10	___	___	___	___	___	___	___	___
• Grade 11	___	___	___	___	___	___	___	___
• Grade 12	___	___	___	___	___	___	___	___

	Language Arts	Math	Social Studies	Science	Foreign Language	Physical Education	Other Elective		Overall School
							Academic Elective	Nonacademic Elective	
N. Collaborative Planning Time[8] (min/week)									
O. Schoolwide Staff Development (days or hours)[9]									
P. Teacher Load									
• Grade 6 or 9[4]	——	——	——	——	——	——	——	——	——
• Grades 7–8 or 10[4]	——	——	——	——	——	——	——	——	——
• Grades 11–12[4]	——	——	——	——	——	——	——	——	——
Q. Percentage of Teachers With Three or Fewer Years of Teaching Experience									
R. Percentage of Certified Teachers									

(Continued)

Figure 6.4 (Continued)

	Language Arts	Math	Social Studies	Science	Foreign Language	Physical Education	Other Elective	Overall School
S. Average Teacher Salary								
• Average special-education teacher salary	___	___	___	___	___	___	___	___
• Average bilingual teacher salary	___	___	___	___	___	___		___

SOURCE: © Education Resource Strategies.

NOTE: Reg Ed = regular education; ELL = English language learner; Spec Ed Res = Special-education resource.

1. The entries here should add up to your school's total enrollment. For example, even though special-education resource students participate in the regular education program, count them here in the special-education resource line. "Self-contained" refers to students who are assigned to usually smaller classrooms that contain students of similar program classification for all or most subjects.

2. The total number of students in all programs (total in Row A) divided by the total number of teachers assigned to the school in all programs (total in Row B).

3. This includes special-education resource students who are integrated most of the time and bilingual students not in separate programs as well as teachers paid for by Title I if they are used schoolwide as regular-classroom teachers.

4. Show grade-level breakouts only if there are significant differences in practice across grades.

5. This includes tutoring or intervention programs as well as required afterschool tutoring or small-group academic work.

6. Estimate based on a typical student schedule.

7. Noninstructional or maintenance time includes homeroom time, advisory time (unless there is a structured curriculum), passing time, lunch, and study periods (unless there is a structured curriculum).

8. Collaborative planning time should include only those instruction-free minutes that are scheduled for groups of teachers to collaborate together. It does not include individual common planning.

9. This refers to time when all teachers have instruction-free time designated for professional development or planning purposes. This might include early release time (if not included above) and staff development days built into the teacher work calendar.

Figure 6.5 Strategic school resource diagnostic tool: How well does your school organize its time, talent, and attention?

Directions: Refer to your Resource Measurement Worksheets to complete the Strategic School Resource Diagnostic Tool. If you don't know an answer, even after completing the preparation worksheet, simply put a question mark. Use Column 3 to document the current status and note key areas for further action or investigation. Although you will identify numerous opportunities for improvement here, you need to match these to your student performance and teacher capacity needs to prioritize.

Resource Principles	Leading Indicators and Questions to Consider	Interpreting the Data and Issues for Investigation
Guiding Resource Strategy 1: Invest in teaching quality through hiring, professional development, job structure, and common planning time		
A. Hire and organize staff to fit school needs in terms of expertise, philosophy, and schedule.	• Use of a strategic, rigorous hiring process ____ Do you have a long-range hiring plan? ____ Do you have written job descriptions specific to each position? ____ Does your school hiring team have a process for evaluating applicants that includes protocol questions and a rubric? ____ Do you require candidates to teach a lesson or have their work evaluated by the hiring team? ____ Have you hired all needed teachers by the summer before the following school year? ____ Have you considered hiring any staff on staggered or part-time schedules to accommodate student needs or school design? ____ Does your school systematically use student teachers or interns as a way to screen potential new hires? • Teacher experience and expertise focused on high-need areas Looking at Rows Q and R on your Resource Worksheet, is there ____ a concentration of novice (less than three years experience) teachers in certain grades or subjects? ____ a difference in teacher qualifications across grades and subject areas?	If your school does not have these components in place, which seem most important for the coming year? Highlight opportunities for improving the expertise in high-needs areas or leveraging teacher expertise more effectively by shifting teachers to new assignments or building new expertise.

(Continued)

109

Figure 6.5 (Continued)

Resource Principles	Leading Indicators and Questions to Consider	Interpreting the Data and Issues for Investigation
	____ a balance of student performance across subjects and grades? ____ Are your most-expert teachers assigned to meet your highest student performance priorities? ____ Do you know the training, experience, and interests of each of your staff members? ____ Have you organized teachers in teams that allow sharing of different skills and expertise?	
B. Integrate significant resources for well-designed professional development that provides expert support to implement the school's core instructional design.	• Professional development aligned with school design and performance priorities ____ Do you use student performance data and analysis of student work to identify priorities for professional development? ____ Do teachers work together to review assessment results and adjust instruction in response? • ____ Do you use a specific reform design, professional development approach, or a literacy/math model that provides protocols and a common language for teacher collaboration around content? • Strategic use of coaches, mentors, lead teachers, and principal/instructional leaders ____ Do you match the expertise of your coaches, lead teachers, and mentors to the prioritized student and teacher needs? ____ Do coaches have the opportunity to observe and work with teachers in their classrooms?	Where do you have opportunities to be more systematic or strategic in using existing resources? High-performing schools use experts to help address their most pressing needs. Such support is most effective when it is given in the context of an individual teacher's classroom and practice. Are you using coaches, mentors, and so forth in a way that maximizes their impact?

Resource Principles	Leading Indicators and Questions to Consider	Interpreting the Data and Issues for Investigation
C. Design teacher work schedules to include blocks of collaborative planning time effectively used to improve classroom practice.	• Collaborative planning time ___ Looking at Row N on your Resource Review Worksheet, do teachers have at least 90 minutes each week to work together to improve instruction? ___ Referring to Row O on your Resource Review Worksheet, are there significant blocks of time (totaling at least 30 hours) throughout the year for the entire teaching staff to work together for schoolwide planning? ___ Do you have a yearlong calendar for professional development that includes all available teacher time for collaboration? • Support and accountability for effective use of common planning time ___ Does each teacher team have clear agendas and protocols for using planning time? ___ Do teacher teams have expert support from lead teachers, coaches, or other instructional leaders? ___ Do you regularly review student performance results by teacher, by teaching team, and by coach (if applicable) to discuss adjustments and support needed?	For collaborative planning time to be effective, teachers need to be able to meet together for at least 90 minutes per week. In addition, you need at least 30 hours per year to do schoolwide planning and professional development. If your school does not yet provide this opportunity, can you find more time for teacher teams to collaborate? Is supporting and ensuring effective collaboration an improvement priority?

(Continued)

Figure 6.5 (Continued)

Resource Principles	Leading Indicators and Questions to Consider	Interpreting the Data and Issues for Investigation
D. Enact systems that promote individual teacher growth through induction, leadership opportunities, professional development planning, evaluation, and compensation.	• ___ Do you have a plan for supporting each teacher new to the school? • ___ Do you and your leadership team develop and review an individual professional development and performance plan with each teacher that informs employment, support, and professional development? • ___ Do teachers have the opportunity to play instructional leadership roles based on proficiency and need? • ___ Can teachers earn additional rewards for high performance or differentiated responsibilities?	Do you need to create a more systematic approach for developing individual teacher skills, especially supporting new teachers?
Guiding Resource Strategy 2: Create individual attention and personal learning environments		
E. Assess student learning to adjust instruction and support.	• Systematic use of formative assessments to guide instruction ___ Do you administer formative assessments to all students that you can compare across classrooms to measure literacy and math attainment throughout the year? ___ Do you have common curriculum goals and assignments in all classrooms across grades so that student work can be reviewed? ___ Do you have time and protocols for reviewing the results together in teacher teams? • Existence of individual student plans and goals ___ Do you have individual plans with learning goals, programs of study, and support strategies for students who fall behind expected levels? ___ Do you have individual plans with learning goals, programs of study, and support strategies for *all* students, including those above expected proficiency levels? ___ Are these plans reviewed regularly throughout the year by teachers and parents?	The key to systemic formative assessment is *using* the data to improve teaching across the school. High-performing schools put the structures and systems in place to help faculty examine student learning and explore how they may adjust their instruction to support further improvement. High-performing schools use individual student plans to help teachers further analyze the needs of students and create more supportive environments for their learning.

112

Resource Principles	Leading Indicators and Questions to Consider	Interpreting the Data and Issues for Investigation
F. Create smaller group sizes and reduce teacher loads in high-need areas.	• Overall class size averages (refer to Resource Review Worksheet rows as follows) Overall school average students per teacher (Row C): ____ Regular-education average class size (Row D) schoolwide: ____ Special-education self-contained (Row G): ____ Bilingual/Limited English Proficient average class size (Row H): ____ Gifted self-contained/Honors/AP (Row I): ____ • Student and teacher program assignment (Elementary only: Rows E and F) Percentage of students in regular-education classrooms: ____ Percentage of teachers who work with regular-education students ____ ____ Do you organize to create smaller group sizes in targeted subject areas? (Elementary schools refer to Rows J and K) ____ Do you allocate resources to provide individual tutoring when needed? • Lower class sizes and teacher loads in early grades. (Row D for elementary; Rows D and P for secondary) K–3 Class size ____ Grades 4–5 Class size ____ Grades 6 Class size ____ Overall teacher load ____ Grades 7–8 Class size ____ Teacher load ____ Grade 9 Class size ____ Teacher load ____	If the difference between your regular-education class size average and the overall school average is more than five, you may be able to create more individual attention in your focus area by rethinking the use of teaching staff, including resource teachers, special subject teachers, as well as teachers who work with students in self-contained classrooms. If the difference between your percentage of teachers and percentage of students in regular-education classrooms is more than 20 percentage points, you may be able to leverage the skills of your special program teachers to support priority skill areas for all students. If class size is the same for early and later grades, you might consider reallocating instructors or regrouping students to create smaller groups in early grades, where research shows that small groups have the most impact. This should always be considered along with teaching quality.

(Continued)

Figure 6.5 (Continued)

Resource Principles	Leading Indicators and Questions to Consider	Interpreting the Data and Issues for Investigation
	• Lower class sizes and teacher loads in English/language arts and math classes. (Secondary schools refer to Rows D and P.) English/language arts class size _____ Math Class size _____ Electives Class size _____ English/language arts teacher load _____ Math teacher load _____ Electives teacher load _____	Strategic schools may choose to lower class size and teacher load in core academic subjects such as language arts and math while maintaining or increasing class size in electives or other academic subjects. Remember, class size reductions don't usually make a huge difference unless group sizes have fewer members than 18 and teaching quality is high.
G. Organize structures that foster personal relationships between students and teachers.	• _____ Do you assign adult advocates or advisors who provide individual academic and personal support usually over several years? • _____ Do you have cluster/houses or teacher teams that share responsibility for common groups of students? • _____ Do you use looping practices—keeping students and teachers together for two or three years in high-need subjects or at critical grade junctures?	Given your other practices for creating individual attention, might any of these foster better relationships in your school?
Guiding Resource Strategy 3: High-performing schools use student time strategically, emphasizing core academics and literacy		
H. Maximize time, including longer blocks of uninterrupted time, that students spend on academic subjects.	• Use of student time (Row M) Weekly minutes in language arts: _____ Weekly minutes in math: _____ Total instructional minutes weekly: _____ Total yearly instructional hours (weekly minutes multiplied by number of weeks): _____	High-performing schools maximize the time that low-performing students spend in English/language arts and math with high-quality instruction.

114

Resource Principles	Leading Indicators and Questions to Consider	Interpreting the Data and Issues for Investigation
	Percentage of student time spent in English/language arts: ____ Percentage of student time in math: ____ Percentage of student time in instruction: ____ ____ Are there ways to extend the school day or year for some or all students? ____ Have you considered ways to increase the percentage of time spent on core academics by changing schedule or program offerings? ● ____ Does your schedule allow for periods of time longer than an hour for students and teachers to engage in activities that may take longer, such as simulations, labs, etc.?	Some high-performing schools schedule regular blocks of time (not necessarily every day) for core subjects such as literacy, math, and other learning activities that may require longer blocks.
I. Vary time and instructional programs to ensure all students meet rigorous academic standards.	● Opportunities for acceleration and remediation (Row L) Maximum minutes of acceleration per week: ____ Maximum minutes of remediation per week: ____	Are there opportunities to extend or differentiate learning opportunities based on student needs?

SOURCE: © Education Resource Strategies.

Figure 6.6 Fleming Teacher Inventory

Grade	Teacher	Certification	Years Teaching (Including This Year)	Content Training (Readers/Writers Workshop; Guiding Reading)	Implementation of Readers/ Writers Workshop	Implementation of TERC Investigations/ Math Curriculum	Math Student Performance Measures (Summary)	Teacher Evaluation Ratings/ Scores (Summary)[b]
K2	Osborne	Early Childhood	3	Partial	Medium	Medium		
K2	Perez[a]	Elem Ed/ELL	7	Partial	Medium	Low		
K2	Blanco	Elem Ed/ELL	21	Partial	Low	Low		
1 (ELL)	Patino	Elem Ed/ELL	5	Complete	High	High	High	Expert
1 (ELL)	Rodriguez[a]	Elem Ed/ELL	15	Complete	High	High	High	Expert
1	Moore	Elem Ed (1–6)	17	Complete	High	Medium	High	Practitioner
1	Martin	Early Child/Elem Ed	16	Complete	High	Medium	High	Expert
2 (ELL)	DiPalma	Elem Ed/ELL	10	Partial	High	Low	Low	Journeyman

Grade	Teacher	Certification	Years Teaching (Including This Year)	Content Training (Readers/Writers Workshop; Guiding Reading)	Implementation of Readers/ Writers Workshop	Implementation of TERC Investigations/ Math Curriculum	Math Student Performance Measures (Summary)	Teacher Evaluation Ratings/ Scores (Summary)[b]
2	Baker	Elem Ed (1–6)	14	Partial	High	Medium	Low	Practitioner
2	Roberts[a]	Elem Ed/ ELL	9	Partial	High	Medium	High	Expert
2	Maxwell	Elem Ed and French (6–12)	10	Partial	Medium	Medium	Low	Journeyman
3 (ELL)	Hernandez	ELL	3	Partial	Low	Medium	Meets	Novice
3	Stewart[a]	Early Childhood PreK–3	5	Partial	Medium	Low	Low	Journeyman
3	Harris	Elem Ed (1–6) and Mild/ Moderate Disabilities (K–8)	2	None	Low	Low	Low	Novice

(Continued)

Figure 6.6 (Continued)

Grade	Teacher	Certification	Years Teaching (Including This Year)	Content Training (Readers/Writers Workshop; Guiding Reading)	Implementation of Readers/ Writers Workshop	Implementation of TERC Investigations/ Math Curriculum	Math Student Performance Measures (Summary)	Teacher Evaluation Ratings/ Scores (Summary)[b]
3	Green	Elem Ed	1	Partial	Medium	Low	Low	Novice
4	Matthews	Elem Ed/ ELL	22	Partial	Low	Low	Meets	Novice
4	Danielson[a]	Elem Ed (1–6)	5	Complete	High	Medium	High	Practitioner
4 (ELL)	Guerra	Elem Ed (1–6)	4	Partial	Medium	Low	Meets	Journeyman
4	Roberts	Elem Ed (1–6)	2	Partial	Medium	Low		Novice
5 (ELL)	Martinez	ELL, K–3, 1–6,	6	Partial	Medium	Medium	Low	Journeyman
5	Collins	Elem Ed (1–6)	16	Partial	Medium	Low	Meets	Journeyman
5	Parker	Elem Ed (1–6)	5	Partial	Medium	Low	Low	Novice

Grade	Teacher	Certification	Years Teaching (Including This Year)	Content Training (Readers/Writers Workshop; Guiding Reading)	Implementation of Readers/ Writers Workshop	Implementation of TERC Investigations/ Math Curriculum	Math Student Performance Measures (Summary)	Teacher Evaluation Ratings/ Scores (Summary)[b]
5	Jones[a]	K–8	10	Complete	High	Medium	High	Expert
Literacy Coach	Estes	Reading: Elem and Middle School	19	Complete	High	N/A		Expert
Reading Recovery	Write	Reading: Elem	4	Complete	N/A			Expert

a. Indicates team leader.

b. As part of the evaluation process in this district, teachers are rated at four levels of proficiency based on student performance and classroom demonstration. These include novice, journeyman, practitioner, and expert.

NOTE: TERC = Technical Education Resource Centers; K = kindergarten; Elem Ed = elementary education; ELL = English-language learners.

How to Group Students and Assign Teachers

7

This chapter describes how to create a strategic plan to group students and assign teachers. It focuses most heavily on strategies to create individual attention that were presented in Chapter 4 and that correspond to Principles E through G in the Strategic School Resource Diagnostic Tool presented in Chapter 6 (pages 112–114).

Each chapter in this implementation section covers a different strategic planning topic. Readers should begin Part III by reading Chapter 6, because it introduces the Fleming case example, including an assessment of Fleming's academic needs. Chapters 7 to 9 can be read in any order. They follow the same basic process for creating a strategic plan:

1. Determine your school's highest-priority academic needs.

2. Assess how well your resources are aligned with your academic needs.

3. Set concrete goals that meet your highest-priority needs.

4. Identify and evaluate options for accomplishing your goals.

5. Create a strategy by choosing a set of options that works for you.

We discuss Step 6, implementation and measurement of progress, in Chapter 10, "Putting It All Together."

STEP 1: DETERMINE YOUR SCHOOL'S HIGHEST-PRIORITY ACADEMIC NEEDS

A strategic staffing and grouping plan builds on a thorough review of student performance priorities by grade, subject, and student subgroup. Recall from Chapter 6 that we summarized the pressing academic needs of Fleming students as follows:

- Math scores started low and declined the longer students stayed in the school.
- Critical thinking and problem solving were weak across the curriculum.
- English/language arts (ELA) student performance did not meet school goals.
- There were no discernible performance differences among the more than 90% of students who were Hispanic or African American based on ethnicity.
- Student performance in the areas of math, English, and critical thinking were uniformly low; there were no students at advanced levels, and few students scored proficient.

STEP 2: ASSESS HOW WELL YOUR RESOURCES ARE ALIGNED WITH YOUR ACADEMIC NEEDS

The Strategic School Resource Diagnostic Tool (see Figure 6.5, Principles E–G, pages 112–114) covers three areas in which we can evaluate how well the Fleming School has organized to provide individual attention. Does the Fleming School

- assess student learning and adjust instruction and support for students accordingly?
- create smaller group sizes and lower teaching loads in areas of highest academic need?
- organize additional structures that foster personal relationships among students and teachers?

Does the Fleming School Assess Student Learning to Adjust Instruction and Support?

As the questions in Principle E suggest, schools that adhere to this principle continuously adjust instruction and support for students based on rigorous assessments of what students have just learned. They do this by administering literacy and math assessments that can be used across the school to determine which students have mastered a particular standard and which have not. They employ common curricula, goals, and assignments across classrooms so that teachers can jointly evaluate student work using well-defined protocols. They create common time for teachers to engage in these team activities. They require teachers to create individual student plans that specify learning goals and support strategies for *all* students, and they review those plans regularly throughout the year.

How does the Fleming School rate? The Fleming School does administer a number of student performance assessments that could be used to guide instruction and grouping. These include a diagnostic reading assessment to measure elementary-grade reading levels and diagnose areas of proficiency as well as "running records" of student progress that K–8 teachers create as they implement the Readers and Writers Workshop. In math, the school uses "Math Investigations" for elementary grades and "Connected Math" for the middle grades.

Although these common assessment tools exist, Fleming teachers implement them inconsistently and do not discuss them in common planning time together. They do not use the assessments to collectively consider ways of grouping students differently to provide individual attention. Fleming School leaders would answer no to all of the questions related to assessment on the Strategic School Resource Diagnostic Tool. Since any grouping strategy must evolve out of this kind of work, the Fleming School should probably choose to set a goal for "improving assessment strategies" when we get to Step 3.

Does the Fleming School Create Smaller Group Sizes and Teacher Loads in High-Need Areas?

The strategic schools we have discussed found ways to free up teachers to work with students in small-group or individual settings. At the secondary level, they also worked to reduce class sizes and teacher loads in high-need areas such as math and literacy. The questions in Strategic School Resource Diagnostic Tool Principle F (page 113) help you evaluate your school's available resources and current practices in these areas.

How would the Fleming School answer these questions? Let's examine the K–5 grades first. Figure 7.1 describes the staffing and grouping arrangements of the Fleming School in Grades K–5.

The Fleming School organizes elementary grades into classes of 20 students. Homeroom teachers teach all academic subjects. Additional

Figure 7.1   Resource review worksheet: Fleming response: Elementary K–5
student enrollment and teaching assignments (Rows A and B in
Figure 6.3, the Resource Measurement Worksheet)

Assignment	Number of Students	Percentage of Students	Number of Teachers	Percentage of Teachers
Homeroom classroom				
Regular-education program (with resource room)	294	65%	16	44%
Special-education self-contained	31	7%	3	8%
Limited-English self-contained	126	28%	7	19%
Subject specialists (art, music, physical education, etc.)			5	14%
Resource teachers				15%
Special-education resource	68[a]	15%[a]	3	
Other resource teachers			1	
Instructional coaches			1.5	
Total	451	100%	36.5	100%

a. As in most schools, special-education resource room students spend most of their time
in regular classrooms. They are listed in both places but only counted once in the
enrollment total.

support is provided to students mostly based on categorical program
designation. Class sizes averages are as follows:

- Regular education: 20
- Special education: 10
- Bilingual: 18

In addition, three special-education resource teachers provide support
to students referred to this program, and there is a reading recovery teacher
who works with six students. This is a significant amount of extra support
for individual attention. In this case, it does not serve Fleming's needs as well
as it could, because these teachers do not serve the majority of students who
might benefit from additional individual attention. Likewise, even for those
students served, the smaller settings are not organized to focus on critical

subject areas (except the reading recovery teacher). Finally, the teachers providing additional support do not coordinate with the homeroom teacher to ensure that the materials and approach of the supplemental instruction align in a way that helps students meet specific standards that they had failed to attain.

At the secondary level, the Fleming School organizes class sizes of 20 in all subjects, including math and English. Teacher load, at slightly more than 80 students per teacher, is lower than seen in many schools and is roughly the same in all subjects, including English and math.

Does the Fleming School Organize Additional Structures That Foster Personal Relationships Among Students And Teachers?

You may want to turn to Principle G in the Strategic School Resource Diagnostic Tool (page 114) and read the questions. As these questions suggest, strategic schools often organize additional structures to foster deeper personal relationships among students and teachers. These include assigning adult advocates or advisors, organizing students into clusters or houses with teams of teachers who share responsibility for common groups of students, and maintaining student-teacher class groupings for more than one year ("looping"). In Chapter 5, we proposed that these strategies are best considered *after* schools have maximized the use of teaching resources to create individual attention around content. Strategic school leaders choose these structures with careful deliberation so that they support the school's vision and overall approach and so that they match the skill set of the existing faculty.

With an enrollment of 752 in Grades K through 8, there are between 80 and 90 students per grade level. As such, the Fleming School is neither large nor small. While the school has no explicit programs for these structures to support more personal relationships, in the absence of a clearly defined instructional approach, it is hard to evaluate which, if any, of these structures would best fit the school's needs.

STEP 3: SET CONCRETE GOALS THAT MEET YOUR HIGHEST-PRIORITY NEEDS

If you have been following along with your own school's data, take a moment to prioritize your school's academic needs and determine whether your current student-teacher groupings are meeting those needs well. Do you have a few students who really need extra help, or does everyone need intense help just to meet standards? Have you already found ways to provide support for college planning but need to consider creating more individual attention in content areas? One way to examine these questions is to use a simple matrix for recording student needs by subject and target group as demonstrated in Figure 7.2. While of course you want to maximize individual attention for everyone, there may be particular groups whose needs demand a higher priority on individual attention than others.

Once you have a clear understanding of priorities for individual attention, set goals for improving individual attention that addresses your own school's needs. Being clear about both the purpose and the target group of individual attention will help you select specific strategies that work for your school.

What Might Fleming Do?

Based on the evaluation of student and teacher needs just described, what goals might Fleming School leaders set for improving individual attention? We suggest that Fleming leaders adopt the following two goals:

1. Improve ability of teachers to systematically measure whether students are learning and mastering standards throughout the year.

2. Provide more attention in the critical subjects of math and English for all students, not just for some. This goal applies to Grades K through 5 and middle-grade students, although we will discuss options and strategies separately.

Figure 7.2 Identify your priorities for individual attention

| Subject | Target Group | | |
	All Students	Underperforming Only	Early Grades Only
English/language arts			
Math			
All subjects			
Study skills			
Community building, social and emotional support			
College admittance			

The first goal requires the Fleming School to create collaborative planning time and to adopt rubrics and student assessment practices described in earlier chapters and again in the next two chapters on creating a master schedule and improving teaching quality.

The second goal is part of the strategy of assigning teachers to student groups and is the focus of this chapter.

STEP 4: IDENTIFY AND EVALUATE
OPTIONS FOR ACCOMPLISHING YOUR GOALS

Our choice to provide more attention in the critical subjects of English and math for all students (Fleming's Goal 2) affects the types of policy options the Fleming might wish to consider. Figure 7.3 illustrates this. It pairs a list of goals with strategies that might address them. Note that while the goals are all similar, the cost of the options can vary profoundly. It presents four basic options for increasing individual attention through a new staffing and grouping plan, each of which could be applied to different groupings of students or for different purposes:

- Reduce class sizes
- Offer teacher-facilitated small-group instruction
- Provide individual tutoring
- Reduce teacher load

Tradeoffs and Considerations

After we discuss the tradeoff and considerations inherent in each of these options generally, we will return to the Fleming case and discuss how the Fleming School might choose among the various options associated with its specific goals.

Option 1: Reduce Class Sizes. Reducing all class sizes is the most common strategy for increasing individual attention. As described in Chapter 5, research suggests that lowering class size does not predictably increase student performance unless class sizes can be as low as 15. Even then, the impact may not be huge. Such large class-size reductions can be very costly. In fact, in most cases, reducing class sizes from 25 to 15 requires a school to double its teaching expenditures.

If you already have class sizes low enough that a small reduction might move classrooms to threshold levels, this could be a feasible strategy. We have seen schools manage this by integrating students and teachers from special programs into the regular classroom or perhaps by

Figure 7.3   Options for providing individual attention through staffing and grouping

Individual Attention Goal	Options to Accomplish Goal
Provide more attention in the critical subjects of math and English for all students, not just for some[a]	• Schoolwide strategy for teacher-facilitated small groups in English/language arts (ELA) and math • Smaller class sizes in all ELA and math classes • Smaller teacher loads for all ELA and math teachers[b]
Increase individual attention in ELA and math (or other priority subjects) for targeted students or student groups	• Teacher-facilitated small groups in some subjects • Resource room study • Smaller class sizes for ELA and math for some students • Smaller teacher loads for ELA and math[b] • Tutoring
Increase individual attention in all subject areas for all students	• Across-the-board class-size reductions • Across-the-board teacher load reduction

a. Refers to strategies more common at the secondary level.

b. Identified as a goal for the Fleming School.

reducing special-subject teachers. This means that all teachers would now need to be skilled in serving a diverse range of student needs and have high levels of instructional expertise in all content areas.

More targeted class-size reductions in certain grades and subjects can be powerful ways to improve student performance. Elementary and secondary schools can fund grade-level class-size reductions by raising class sizes in other grades. Of course, schools choosing this strategy would need to ensure that students mastered needed skills in the early grades to enable teachers with larger class sizes to be effective in later grades.

At the secondary level, school leaders may find it feasible to reduce class sizes only in targeted subject areas. The school might have the ability to fund the needed teachers by raising class sizes in other subject areas, like physical education, where small class size is not as critical to meeting learning objectives.

Option 2: Offer Teacher-Facilitated Small-Group Instruction. While creating smaller class sizes in subjects like ELA and math can be a strategic way to target individual attention at the secondary level, targeting by subject can be more difficult in elementary schools, where typically one teacher teaches all subjects. Many teachers use grouping strategies in their own classrooms and rotate to facilitate these groups. However, this may not provide enough focused, continuous attention to fully support these students. As described in Chapter 5, many high-performing schools "push" expert reading teachers into regular classrooms for 45 to 90 minutes each day or every other day for literacy instruction. Clearly, this can be a more affordable strategy for many schools.

Pushing experts into regular classrooms for small-group work requires that the school be able to find sufficient experts to implement such a strategy. If so, this strategy has the potential added benefit of building the capacity of the regular-education classroom teacher by exposing him or her to new techniques and creating joint responsibility for student reading performance.

Option 3: Individual Tutoring. As discussed in Chapter 5, individual tutoring, effectively implemented, can achieve powerful results. But implementing tutoring can mean devoting significant resources to a small number of students. This may make sense in cases in which performance analysis shows the need for extra support in specific skill areas or for a small number of students for a short period of time. Many high-performing schools strategically combine tutoring with other individual attention strategies, such as rigorous formative assessment, to enable students to succeed in small- and large-group settings.

Option 4: Reducing Teacher Load. Reducing teacher load (the number of students assigned to a teacher) usually only applies to the secondary level, where loads can reach more than 150 students each semester. Unlike class-size reduction, reducing teaching load is not expensive—or at least it doesn't have to be. It can be a cost-effective strategy for increasing individual attention, especially in subjects like ELA and math, where teachers need to spend significant time providing feedback to students. Teachers with smaller student loads can also get to know their students in different ways.

Two common ways to reduce teaching load are to reduce class sizes or to add a planning period so that teachers teach one fewer course per day without changing the schedule. Both of these options are very expensive ways to reduce teacher load.

Less costly ways to reduce teaching load include

- **Combining subjects** like English and social studies. Instead of teaching four cohorts of students for four periods, teachers would teach only two cohorts, each for double blocks. In this example, teacher load would be reduced in half.

- **Semesterizing courses** and doubling the time students spend in them each week. This might mean that students would take a double block of math one semester and a double block of social studies the next semester. This example would also reduce teacher load in half for that point in time, but the next semester, the teacher would be responsible for a new set of students and their learning.
- **Increasing the percentage of time** spent on target subjects. For example, students would take two periods of English each day and one period of all other subjects. This would reduce teacher load for only English teachers.

While these ways of reducing teacher load are less expensive, they do require tradeoffs. Teachers require additional subject specialization and, on average, will have less subject expertise when subjects are combined. Also, increasing the percentage of time spent in target subjects reduces time spent in other subjects for a school day of a given length.

What Might Fleming Do?

Because Fleming is attempting to raise the performance of nearly all of its students, it will probably consider options to create small groups in ELA and math at the elementary school level and to reduce ELA and math class sizes. It could consider reducing teacher loads at the secondary level, but teaching loads of 80 are already fairly low compared with many locations, so this should only be considered if there is a compelling reason to expect that combining subjects will have a big impact on student performance.

If you have not already done so, remind yourself of what your school is trying to accomplish, and take a moment to decide which options might be most applicable for your own school.

STEP 5: CREATE A STRATEGY BY CHOOSING A SET OF OPTIONS THAT WORKS FOR YOU

The next step to creating a staffing and grouping strategy is to choose between the available options and decide how much to invest with any given option (e.g., how much to reduce a literacy group size). To determine the combination of options that make sense in your context, you'll use your own judgment to weigh each option's expected impact on student performance against its feasibility. Whether a policy option is feasible will depend on the policy's cost, its alignment with other approaches, your school's current capacity, and the barriers to implementation.

Is a Policy Feasible for Your School?

- **Costs**—How do the costs stack up to the expected benefits?
- **Alignment**—Does the policy support other instructional approaches?
- **Capacity**—Do your current teachers have the capacity and expert resources available to address new professional development needs?
- **Implementation barriers**—Do district, regulatory, or contractual policies, or lack of ownership by staff, prevent you from implementing now?

Figure 7.4 summarizes the considerations reviewed previously for each strategy and outlines the conditions that indicate whether this strategy might be a good fit for your student performance needs, student population mix, resource levels, and teacher capacity.

What Might Fleming Do?

Given the large number of students who need improvement in literacy and math, we suggest that Fleming consider a strategy for creating teacher-facilitated small-group instruction in ELA and math in the elementary grades as well as a strategy to reduce class sizes in ELA or math in the middle-school grades. A small-group strategy could be funded by cross-training already existing resource teachers in literacy and math and supporting them as they work with resource students in content areas in their regular classrooms in small-group settings. Other resource-neutral options are to free up resources for small groups by raising class sizes in one or more grades and exchanging a homeroom teacher for an itinerant reading or math specialist who works with children in small groups.

Questions still remain. How, for instance, do we evaluate the potential impact of creating small groups for students against the potential impact of, say, hiring a coach to work with struggling teachers? How does that compare to creating collaborative time for teachers to learn from each other? At this point in the strategic planning process, we can rule out individual attention strategies that seem unlikely to meet the needs of the Fleming School, but until we examine the needs and the options across the other components of our resource strategy—creating a master schedule and plan to improve teaching quality—covered in Chapters 8 and 9, it is hard to make final decisions about what ought to be done in the Fleming case. In Chapter 10, we discuss the interaction of choices made or considered as part of the staffing and grouping strategy with changes to the master schedule and the professional development strategy.

Figure 7.4   Summary selection considerations

Typical Strategy	Selection Considerations	Strategic Fit When . . .
For All Schools		
Across-the-board class-size reduction.	• No specific content area targeted. • No specific student groups targeted. • Can be expensive to reduce class sizes to low-enough levels. • Assumes all teachers have a high level of teacher capacity in priority areas.	• Student needs are distributed evenly across grades and subject. • Sufficient resources exist to reduce class sizes to 15 or fewer. • Teacher capacity is uniformly high.
Teacher-facilitated small-group instruction for all students in English/language arts (ELA) or math.	• Cost depends on target size of small groups and number of classrooms. • Requires highly expert teachers to facilitate small-group instruction in ELA and math.	• All students need support in specific subject areas. • Resources can be freed to support expert teachers. • Need to build overall teaching capacity in ELA or math.
Small-group instruction only for under-performing students in resource room settings.	• Cost-intensive for small number of students served. • Requires expert tutors.	• Only a few students in each classroom need intensive support. • Resource support can be scheduled in ways that don't disrupt student's participation in regular classroom. • Limited teacher capacity to serve diverse learning needs exists.
Individual tutoring for underperforming students.	• Cost depends on number of students receiving tutoring as well as duration and frequency of tutoring.	• Few students need intensive support to reach standards.
Secondary-School Specific		
Smaller class sizes for some subjects.	• Cost depends on number of subjects and grades.	• Resource levels allow significant reduction in targeted areas.

(Continued)

Figure 7.4 (Continued)

Typical Strategy	Selection Considerations	Strategic Fit When . . .
	• Requires all teachers in that subject to have high levels of capacity to use smaller class sizes in ways that improve student performance.	• Class sizes can be raised in other subject areas. • Teacher capacity in target area is high. • Resource levels are low; class sizes are high.
Smaller teacher loads for some subjects.	• Is ongoing cost-neutral for most implementation strategies. • May reduce time in other subject areas. • May require combining subject areas. • Requires high level of teacher capacity in subject areas or requires teaching combined subjects.	• In transition years between elementary and secondary schools. • When focus is on building literacy skills.

Implementation Challenges and Feasibility

As part of evaluating the feasibility of the various options, you will need to consider contractual, regulatory, or district policy constraints to implementation. If you are confident that your chosen strategy makes sense for students and teachers in your school, then you will want to identify these constraints so you can find ways to mitigate them. Some constraints exist for a reason; these types of constraints will highlight implementation details you should be paying more attention to. We typically find that most school leaders can make a powerful strategy work. To succeed, however, they have to articulate a clear vision about how the new staffing and grouping strategy will benefit students. Proactively identifying and collaborating with likely "enforcers" of the constraints often heightens the chance of success. The most common constraints to the individual attention strategies outlined come in three areas:

- District- or contractually defined class-size and teacher load maximums
- Certification requirements that define which teachers can teach which students and subjects
- Individualized education plans (IEPs) for special-education students

Since individual attention strategies aim largely to create smaller group sizes for some subjects with a fixed set of resources, the challenges arise because group sizes *rise* at other times of the day for other purposes. For example, at the middle-school level, to reduce class size in English classes, you may need to raise class sizes in history above the contractual maximum. Even if the increased class size doesn't surpass contractually defined guidelines, you'll want to consider ways you can support or change the job of teaching history to make it more doable. Should more of the writing occur in English? Should you focus especially on finding student teachers to support history teachers?

Certification requirements can be tricky, especially in the era of the No Child Left Behind Act, when not having the right levels of certification can result in lost funds. Some schools, when they inventory their staff certification areas, are surprised to find that many teachers already have the credentials they need or nearly have the course credits required. A school can phase in a strategy by implementing it as certification requirements are met and by finding ways to support and encourage teachers to become certified. Some schools we have worked with use local universities to provide on-the-job certification while teachers learn new roles in their classrooms. Job descriptions should be rewritten so that all new hires come equipped with the needed skills and certifications.

Reconsidering the ways of providing support to students with special-education needs strikes fear into the hearts of many school leadership teams. There is a sense of mystery and "untouchability" that surrounds the IEP that squashes creative thinking before it begins. Educators have learned the hard way that the consequence of making a mistake can be severe—requiring hours of hassle and costly lawsuits. Because of this, central office leaders can be legalistic and compliance focused in their response to new ways of organizing to meet these students' needs. Clearly, figuring how best to serve students with special-education needs is a complicated business. It requires expert support.

However, having worked with educators who are nationally known for their expertise in special education, we have been reminded that the IEP is just documentation of a plan to respond to each student's needs. Furthermore, federal law specifies that student needs be served in the "least restrictive environment" possible. Over and over again, we see expert principals and leadership teams creating IEPs for special-education students that specify that they be served in a regular classroom setting—being clear about the strategies the teacher will use to do this. The key to success is making sure that teachers *do* have the tools and support they need to be successful with these students.

The individual attention strategies discussed in this chapter cannot be made in isolation, without reference to your instructional approach, your teacher strengths, and your master schedule. Creating a team of itinerant reading specialists, for example, might require creating a master schedule that has blocks for literacy that rotate at different times over the day by grade. Other approaches might work better if all literacy classes were taught in the morning. The choices of staffing and grouping strategies inform the goals and priorities for your master schedule, which we discuss in the next chapter—and vice versa.

How to Craft a Master Schedule That Works

8

Administrators frequently ask us to help them build school schedules. Many of them seem on a quest for a "silver bullet" schedule that solves all of their instructional and logistical problems. While we wish we could craft such a perfect schedule, our usual response is that a school's master schedule will never succeed in addressing the needs of *all* students and faculty members. What we've learned from the principals of strategic schools is that a more realistic measure of the success of a school schedule is not that it accomplishes *all* things, but that it accomplishes the *right* things. In other words, the schedule should be crafted to meet the highest-priority needs of the school's students and faculty.

Each chapter in this implementation section covers a different strategic planning topic. Readers should begin Part III by reading Chapter 6, because it introduces the Fleming case example, including an assessment of Fleming's academic needs. Chapters 7 through 9 can be read in any order. They follow the same basic process for creating a strategic plan:

1. Determine your school's highest-priority academic needs.

2. Assess how well your resources are aligned with your academic needs.

3. Set concrete goals that meet your highest-priority needs.

4. Identify and evaluate options for accomplishing your goals.

5. Create a strategy by choosing a set of options that works for you.

We discuss Step 6, implementation and measurement of progress, in Chapter 10, "Putting It All Together."

The key to creating a successful master schedule is to be clear about what your highest priorities are and then to allocate time and expertise to address those priorities. In practice, that means that each school's optimal schedule will be unique. After all, all schools have a unique constellation of resources, needs, expertise, talent, curricula, and instructional vision. Indeed, as we researched this book, some of the most successful principals we interviewed adjusted their bell schedules every year to adapt to continually changing situations as well as to incorporate lessons learned.

STEP 1: DETERMINE YOUR SCHOOL'S HIGHEST-PRIORITY ACADEMIC NEEDS

Recall from Chapter 6 that we summarized the pressing academic needs of Fleming students as follows:

- Math scores started low and declined the longer students stayed in school.
- Critical thinking and problem solving were weak across the curriculum.
- English/language arts (ELA) student performance did not meet school goals.
- There were no discernible performance differences among the more than 90% of students who were Hispanic or African American based on ethnicity.
- Student performance in the areas of math, English, and critical thinking were uniformly low; there were no students at advanced levels, and few students scored proficient.

STEP 2: ASSESS HOW WELL YOUR RESOURCES ARE ALIGNED WITH YOUR ACADEMIC NEEDS

If there is not one perfect schedule that works for all schools, how do we evaluate whether the use of time aligns with goals in a particular school context? We recommend that you look at Principles H and I of your Strategic School Resource Diagnostic Tool in Chapter 6 (pages 114–115) and consider the following:

- How do students spend time in your school?
  - How much time is spent on instruction (minutes and percentage of overall time)?
  - How much time is spent in English?
  - In math?

- Given student performance in ELA and math, do you need to adjust your schedule to allow more or less time in those subjects?
- Have you considered ways to vary amount and percentage of time in particular subjects to support a particular group of students or pedagogical strategy?

Answering these questions will help you determine how effectively your current practices address your priority needs. A serious diagnostic exercise is a precursor to custom designing an effective school schedule.

As in the last chapter, we will use the example of the Fleming School to discuss the process of building your school schedule. Consider the Fleming School's middle schedule for Grades 6 to 8 shown in Figure 8.1. Middle-school students attend six 55-minute periods each day. Two of these periods are "enrichments," one of which is physical education (PE), and the other of which is arts, music, or computers. For the other four periods, students see four different teachers for daily periods of English, math, science, and social studies. In addition, students have a 20-minute lunch.

Figure 8.1   Middle-school schedule at Fleming School

Fleming School Planning and Class Stated Schedule		Fleming School Planning and Class Realistic Schedule	
Student classes/day	6	Student classes/day	6
Teacher classes/day	4	Teacher classes/day	4
Required team planning sessions/week	1	Required team planning sessions/week	1
Minutes/class average	55	Minutes/class average	55
Passing periods	0	Passing periods	7
Length of passing periods	0	Length of passing periods	5
Noncourse periods (lunch and homeroom)	2	Noncourse periods (lunch and homeroom)	2
Length of noncourse periods	30	Length of noncourse periods	30
Plan/day	1	Plan/day	1
Plan/week	5	Plan/week	5
Percentage of team planning sessions	20%	Percentage of team planning sessions	20%
Planning minutes/day	55	Planning minutes/day	55
Planning minutes/week	275	Planning minutes/week	275
Total minutes/day	360	Total minutes/day	360
Noninstructional minutes/day (students)	30	Noninstructional minutes/day (students)	75
Instructional minutes/day	330	Instructional minutes/day	285
Percentage of day noninstructional time	**8%**	**Percentage of day noninstructional time**	**21%**

Time on Instruction

Note that according to the schedule, there is no passing time between classes. Realistically, though, it takes at least five minutes for students to transfer between classes and lunch. Thus, at best, the instructional time is six 50-minute periods. In addition, sixth period has to end 10 minutes early for students to return to their homerooms, collect their belongings, and get down to the buses. So in reality, students spend 79% of their day on instruction and 21% of the day in noninstructional time.

Varying Time in Subjects to Meet Needs

As shown, each period lasts 50 minutes and does not vary by subject or student. Meanwhile, students at Fleming have challenges with math and ELA content and appear to need accelerated opportunities in these subjects.

Common Planning Time

Teachers do not have 90 minutes of common planning time each week—in fact, the teachers do not have this time set aside at all. Instead, each teacher has one planning period per day and one administrative period to cover activities like lunch, buses, and hallway patrol.

STEP 3: SET CONCRETE GOALS THAT MEET YOUR HIGHEST-PRIORITY NEEDS

Using your findings from your resource reviews and knowledge about your student performance data, identify the goals and priorities you have for your schedule. For example, a review of the Fleming School's data seems to suggest that the school should schedule more time for core academics and for teachers to collaborate and plan together. If we were the principals of Fleming, we might set the following five goals for the Fleming schedule:

- Increase collaborative planning time for grade-level teams to work on ELA and math together
- Increase total instructional time
- Increase time devoted to ELA, especially for struggling students
- Increase time devoted to math, especially for struggling students
- Create a schedule that supports more individual attention in ELA by being compatible with teacher-supported flexible grouping

STEP 4: IDENTIFY AND EVALUATE OPTIONS FOR ACCOMPLISHING YOUR GOALS

Once you're clear on what you want your school's schedule to accomplish, the next step is to examine different ways of meeting your goals through your schedule. Figure 8.2 illustrates several different scheduling strategies high-performing schools have used to accomplish the goals listed previously.

Goal 1. Increase Common Planning Time

Common or collaborative planning time is one of the first reforms many high-performing schools adopt and is an excellent place to begin

Figure 8.2   Five scheduling goals and strategies for meeting them

Common Schedule Goal	Strategic Schedule Design Options
Goal 1. Increase planning time.	• Create double periods. • Combine professional development period with other noninstructional time. • Combine classes for specialist subjects. • Rethink use of student time—alternatives to classroom instruction that free up teacher time for planning (internships, projects, service, etc.). • Reduce teacher administration assignments.
Goal 2. Increase instructional time.	• Reduce maintenance time (homeroom, passing, lunch, and dismissal). • Push noninstructional activities outside of the school day. • Extend the school day (or year).
Goal 3. Increase time in math or English/ language arts (ELA).	• Require additional courses in the priority subject. • Block schedule to create double periods in these subjects. • Adopt literacy or math across the curriculum.
Goal 4. Reduce teaching load.	• Block schedule so teachers teach longer periods and see a smaller number of students. • Create core classes such as humanities by having one teacher teach both ELA and social studies and another teach both math and science; teachers would then be responsible for a smaller number of students.
Goal 5. Vary time based on student need.	• Vary length of classes based on student need. • Create classes with content specific to student need—for example, a ninth-grade reading class that is required in addition to the regular ELA class.

thinking about the design of a new master schedule. As mentioned earlier, high-performing schools tend to structure and organize collaborative teacher time to jointly review student work and to adjust lesson plans by sharing practices that work. Schools have done this by using one or more of seven common strategies (French, Atkinson, & Rugen, 2007; Miles, 2001; Miles & Darling Hammond, 1997; C. Murphy, 1997; Raywid, 1993).

Before we discuss these strategies for the Fleming School, which has no collaborative time for teachers, we invite you to take a moment and consider your own school's current use of common planning time by reviewing the Strategic School Resource Diagnostic Tool, Principle C, in Chapter 6 (page 111). Then as we discuss each strategy, we also hope that you reflect on which of these strategies, if any, might work in your own school to help you increase or improve your use of collaborative planning time for teacher teams.

a. **Create double planning periods** two or three times a week for teams. This strategy puts two "free" or nonteaching periods back to back. Most schools give teachers at least one individual planning period each day, although some elementary teachers only have three sessions per week. Double-blocked planning periods can be created either by adding planning time (a second period per day) or by moving an existing planning session from one day to another day. Changing the use of a personal planning period often requires active faculty and union cooperation and so should be considered in partnership with faculty leaders.

b. **Combine planning period with other noninstructional time** by placing or concentrating planning sessions next to activities such as lunch or before-school and afterschool teacher work time. This strategy can turn a 40-minute planning session into an 80-minute session. Because this strategy concentrates planning time for teachers at certain times of the day, it often forces schools to think creatively about how to "cover" teacher planning time. For example, most elementary schools use full-time subject specialists, like PE, music, and art teachers, to create planning time for teachers. But a schedule that requires coverage for half of all teachers around lunchtime would demand more than the school's allotted number of specialists. To cover this peak in demand, schools we have worked with have used part-time staff or other nonunion contractors who bring special talents to students during these extended blocks of time.

c. **Combine classes** for specialist subjects to create free time for small teaching teams. Schools that cannot find money to add "coverage teachers" to cover increased planning time often find other creative ways to support teachers. For instance, they may allot more time to art, music, and PE (and other elective courses) and then raise class sizes in those important subjects to finance the additional investment. For example, a school that has 60 first-graders, organized into three homeroom classes of 20 students each, might send them to an extended block of art and music (class sizes of 30) on one day and an extended block of music and PE (class sizes of 30) on another day, and so forth. The increase in class size funds a proportional increase in time in subject.

d. **Rethink the use of student time** by creating time for learning activities not supervised by core teachers. These could be internships, community service blocks, weekly "specials-day" theme projects, or study halls. Just because teachers do not directly supervise students during a period of time doesn't mean students aren't learning. A number of schools we have worked with create regular learning opportunities for students in which students are supervised by noninstructional personnel. However, creating and supervising these activities still requires money to hire staff, develop materials, and administer the program, so schools using this strategy will usually need to find dollars somewhere.

e. **Shorten instructional time on one day of the week and add a few minutes to other days.** This strategy is often called "banked time." Holding school a few minutes longer on a daily basis and then releasing 90 or so minutes early on a weekly or biweekly basis can provide additional time for extended sessions of teacher collaboration. Many districts—hundreds of them by our estimate—use this strategy districtwide, with "early release" day each Wednesday, for example. The district then increases the length of the student day by a few minutes for the rest of the days. Schools in districts without an early-release day might find ways to implement such a strategy on their own (although busing can be an issue), or they might use a modified approach. For example, Boston Arts Academy, a secondary school we have discussed several times, creates one longer teacher planning period every Monday, shortening all other periods on that day only. During the common planning time, students have an open period for study, which reduces the need for "coverage" teachers (Shields & Miles, 2008). On the other hand, because all teachers have time off simultaneously, it can be difficult to support teacher teams to ensure that banked time is spent to maximum effect. Banked time is most effective in schools where teacher capacity is already high and teacher teams are already functioning well.

f. **Add time to the teacher work calendar.** Nationwide, the typical student day averages about 6.5 hours, and teacher workdays are typically contractually only slightly longer. Similarly, the typical number of student school days ranges from 180 to 187 days with teachers required to work an additional 2 to 10 days a year. Many districts, like New York City in its most recent contract negotiation, are adding time to the teacher calendar either by lengthening each school day or by adding workdays to the school year. Increasing numbers of public schools are finding ways to do this on their own. Charter schools, too, can usually define their own teacher calendars and workdays. A recent study by the Center for Collaborative Education (2001) found that the most frequent difference between regular Boston Public Schools and those schools with freedom from the teacher contract was in the work schedules. Even in schools without such freedom, however, leaders find ways to change expectations regarding the teaching schedule. These leaders also find creative ways to compensate teachers for this time. For instance, some leaders pay teachers stipends for additional time, while others are able to award professional development credit to teachers who participate in ongoing professional development and collaborative work.

g. **Reduce teacher administrative assignments.** When budgets get tight, schools often think to save money by assigning certified teachers to hallway patrol, lunch monitoring, and other administrative duties. By assigning these duties to paraprofessionals or administrative personnel, schools can often free up large blocks of time for teacher collaboration.

What Might Fleming Do?

In the case of the Fleming school, the school has no real collaboration time but is already investing in a great deal of nonstudent time for teachers—two periods per day on a six-period schedule—which means that teachers are relieved of student duty for a third of the day. Fleming has plenty of potential planning time that just needs to be realized. First, by reducing administrative assignments, even slightly, Fleming can potentially free up hundreds of minutes of time for collaboration. Often, paraprofessionals or other school administrators can take on these assignments on days when teachers have team meetings.

The second issue Fleming needs to address is logistical. How do they get teams of teachers off at the same time? Also, how do they turn short class periods into sessions long enough for meaningful teacher collaboration? (We recommend 90 minutes but have seen 60- to 70-minute sessions also be effective). By assigning teams the same period free and by placing this free time in slots near the beginning of school, the end of school, or before or after lunch, the school could achieve multiple blocks of collaborative planning time each week. Other possible strategies for ensuring that planning sessions are of sufficient length include changing the middle-school bell schedule (block scheduling) or otherwise double-blocking the planning sessions by creative coverage strategies. There are many other options open to the Fleming school. In fact, the options are almost limitless. It is, as always, a matter of tradeoffs and choices.

Choices and Tradeoffs

Like any resource reallocation, each of these strategies introduces choices and tradeoffs. For example, in some schools (not Fleming), creating double planning periods could mean that some teachers don't have planning time each day. Likewise, combining classes for special subjects means that they will have larger class sizes. Concentrating planning time at certain points in the day means that elementary schools may have to hire twice as many part-time staff instead of hiring a few full-time subject specialists. In some situations, professional development days or early release days can be easier to implement than common planning time. While these days have the potential to be useful, the reality is that teacher teams are often unable to have the benefit of expert content support (e.g., one literacy coach cannot possibly attend all of the literacy team meetings in a school if they happen simultaneously). This can lead to inexpertly run meetings that waste valuable teacher time and ultimately lower expectations about the quality of the collaboration, leading to frustration, anger, and ultimately, failure.

On the other hand, with the proper support, as teachers begin to engage in working and learning together to improve student performance, they often demand more time for collaboration. Success or even perceived success can mitigate some of the very real tradeoffs faced by school leaders and teachers, but the tradeoffs still exist, and the onus for making tough decisions falls on school leaders. Leaders seeking to implement collaborative planning time need to weigh the available options and decide what works best for their unique situation.

Goal 2. Increase Instructional Time

As discussed in Chapter 5, high-performing schools schedule to maximize their time on instruction. This can be very important for schools with either short school days (of less than six hours) or significant numbers of students performing several years behind grade level, as is the case with Fleming. There are three common strategies high-performing schools use to increase time on instruction: reducing maintenance time, lengthening student day, and lengthening school year.

a. **Reduce maintenance time.** Some schools increase overall time on instruction by decreasing the amount of time students spend in maintenance activities, such as passing time, homeroom, lunch, and dismissal time. These minutes are then reallocated to instruction. At the elementary level, maintenance time is primarily a function of lunch, recess, homeroom time, and whatever passing is done between homeroom and specials. Elementary schools have attempted to minimize maintenance time by

- Encouraging students to arrive at school and enter classrooms 20 to 30 minutes before the first bell to put away bags, read school announcements, sign in for attendance, turn in homework or other parental communications, and share a few minutes of time with the teacher
- Making announcements during lunch, recess, passing, or other nonacademic time and never during instructional time
- Shortening homeroom time

Figure 8.3 illustrates how the choice of periods per day can affect maintenance time at the secondary level. The column on the right is a "block" schedule in which students attend four longer classes each day. Notice that the number of passing minutes per day and week is significantly shorter in the block schedule. This reduces maintenance time. Also, many schools on six- or seven-period bell schedules dedicate an entire period for lunch, while most four-block schedules have a half-period or shortened time for lunch. Schools that choose to shorten lunch and reduce passing periods can reduce maintenance time from 24% to 18% of the student day or less.

b. **Push noninstructional activities outside of the school day.** A second way to increase the amount of time devoted to instruction is to reduce the amount of school time devoted to other activities such as support and enrichment or pupil services. Often, this is accomplished through the use of outside partnerships that provide afterschool support for students, allowing more of the school day to be focused on instructional activities.

Figure 8.3   Comparison of maintenance time in three prototypical schedules

Prototypical Bell Schedule	Six Periods	Seven Periods	4 × 4 or 4 A/B[a]
Period length (minutes)	50	43	80
Number of passing periods per day	5	6	3
Passing time (minutes per day)	30	36	18
Passing time (minutes per week)	150	180	90
Passing time as percentage of time at school	8%	9%	5%
Lunch time (minutes per day)	50	43	40
Total maintenance time (min/day)	**92**	**91**	**70**
Total maintenance as percentage of day	**24%**	**23%**	**18%**

a. 4 × 4 Schedule: In this schedule, students take four classes every day for the first semester, and then in the second semester, take a different set of four classes every day. For example, students might attend a math, science, history, and physical education class every day in the first semester, and then take English/language arts, art, writing, and economics each day in the second semester. 4 A/B Schedule: In this schedule, students take four longer classes on "A" days and then alternate to take four different and equally long classes on "B" days.

NOTE: This figure assumes a day with seven hours between arrival and dismissal, which is close to the national average; it also assumes that the day is broken into the number of student periods, plus one lunch session. Passing periods are assumed to be six minutes long.

c. **Extend the school day or year.** A third way to increase instructional time is simply to extend the day or year, the "time at school" of students. When maintenance time and support and enrichment time are already low or when such activities are a core part of a school's mission, this may be the only way to increase instructional time.

What Might Fleming Do?

In this case, Fleming already spends a good deal of its time on instructional activities. Even in our "realistically" stated schedule, Fleming spends only 21% of its time in maintenance, largely by virtue of its very short combined lunch and homeroom period of 30 minutes and its lack of any support and enrichment activities in the stated schedule. We will hold in reserve the idea of implementing a block schedule for Fleming. A block schedule would reduce maintenance time by cutting the number of passing periods.

However, the primary goals of a block schedule are usually to create more useful time for learning and to reduce teaching load, neither of which are huge priorities here.

Choices and Tradeoffs

There are, of course, tradeoffs to increasing instructional time. For example, the benefit to reducing maintenance time is not always clear. In some cases, especially where "time at school" is very short, schools may be able to reclaim this time to provide collaborative planning time for teachers or to extend the school day. In other cases, this is not possible, is not needed, or could provoke faculty opposition, depending on the context.

Similarly, support and enrichment activities are an important part of the social and emotional development of children, and it is important not to devalue or underinvest in these activities. For instance, many high-performing schools have implemented advisory or other enrichment programs that have become a vital part of their improvement plan.

At first glance, extending the school day may not appear to entail the same compromises as reducing maintenance or pushing support and enrichment outside of the school day. However, because the resources spent to increase instruction time could be used for other activities, trade-offs are still real, and alternate uses of resources (professional development expenditures, for instance) should always be weighed against the cost of adding time to the school day.

Before considering any of these options, school leaders should carefully consider the impact the change will have on the faculty and the student body. It is rarely a bad idea to integrate teacher leaders in the process of designing a new schedule.

Goal 3. Devote More of Instructional Time to Math or ELA

We have just discussed ways to increase instructional time. Within a fixed amount of instructional time, it is possible to shift time to core academics. While this is not always a desirable strategy, many struggling schools do need to allocate a disproportionate amount of time to math and English. Other schools have a specific focus (such as math, science, technology, or the arts) and may wish to allocate a disproportionate amount of time to another subject. The high-performing schools we studied increased time in math or ELA using two primary strategies: by requiring additional courses for graduation or by enacting a block or other nontraditional schedule.

a. **Change promotion and graduation requirements** or courses offered to force students to spend more time in targeted subjects. For example, some schools mandate four years of core academic subjects for graduation even when district graduation requirements mandate only two or three years of, for instance, math or science.

b. **Use a block schedule to create extended literacy or math sessions.** We have already discussed how elementary schools create extended literacy blocks. Because elementary school teachers have a great deal of freedom to determine how they spend time each day, it is rarely difficult to organize a literacy or math block, although logistically it can be challenging to simultaneously create uninterrupted blocks for literacy, math, and collaborative planning time in all grades.

In secondary schools, the choice of bell schedule can have a tremendous impact on the school's ability to create extended blocks. Figure 8.4 shows the relationship between the bell schedule and the percentage of time in core academic and other subjects, using Fleming as an example.

Figure 8.4 provides one example of what could happen to Fleming with a six-period, seven-period, or four-block bell schedule. In this example, the six-period schedule represents a scenario in which all students take one course in each of the standard six subjects of ELA, math, science, social studies, electives, and PE. This is very similar to Fleming's middle-school schedule. Notice that each student's time divides evenly at 17% in every subject. Schools that want to require students to spend more time in English or math must take away an elective period for those students in the traditional six-period day. While many schools do this, taking away art and music electives from students has many ramifications that should be considered.

In the seven-period-day column (center), we are asking the Fleming school to deliberately assign all students to spend the extra "seventh" period in ELA. Instead of spending 17% of instructional time in every subject, Fleming students now spend 28% of their time in ELA (or another subject if desired) and 14% in all other subjects.

In the eight-period example (usually organized as four classes per day on alternating days), we have assigned all students to take an extra course in English and an extra course in math, so that 50% of each Fleming student's instructional time is spent on ELA and math. Notice that in this example, the student is able to focus on English and math without losing the option to take electives and other courses. This same example holds for any other subjects a school might wish to prioritize.

Figure 8.4   The number of periods and academic time—hypothetical schedule for the Fleming Middle School

Subject	Six Periods per Day		Seven Periods per Day		4 x 4 or 4 A/B	
	Periods	Percentage of Time	Periods	Percentage of Time	Periods	Percentage of Time
English	1	17%	2	28%	2	25%
Social studies	1	17%	1	14%	1	13%
Math	1	17%	1	14%	2	25%
Science	1	17%	1	14%	1	13%
Elective 1	1	17%	1	14%	1	13%
Elective 2	1	17%	1	14%	1	13%

What Might Fleming Do?

While just about any schedule could be made to work and work well, the authors would strongly consider the 4 A/B day for Fleming Middle School unless we discovered complicating factors (such as no support for teachers to learn how to use longer blocks of time or significant faculty or parental opposition). The 4 A/B block schedule allows Fleming to devote more time to both literacy and math, which in this case are both areas of high need, without sacrificing a rich program in arts and music and other elective courses. Because Fleming already invests in two planning periods for its teachers, it will not cost additional money to implement the block schedule and, in fact, is negligibly less expensive. It also has other benefits that we will discuss momentarily (such as reduced teacher load) that help sway us toward the 4 A/B schedule. Again, just about any of these schedules could be modified to meet Fleming's needs. It is all about tradeoffs.

Choices and Tradeoffs

The obvious tradeoff for increasing the percentage of instructional time devoted to math or ELA is that it requires a school to devote less of its instructional time to other subjects. In some cases, this is not desirable or appropriate. Remember also that block scheduling is not always associated with higher-quality instruction. Teachers accustomed to a career of teaching in 50-minute sessions almost certainly need support to learn how to successfully engage students for extended periods of time or in experiential learning activities. Also, a curriculum and set of lesson plans that were designed for 50-minute lessons would probably need significant revision to be appropriate for a block-scheduled school. In some cases, a block schedule cannot be adopted without a faculty vote, which does not always go in favor of block scheduling. In other cases (although not Fleming) adopting a block schedule doubles the amount of teachers' planning time and results (all other things equal) in either an increase in class sizes or the need for additional teachers to cover the additional courses the new bell schedule requires. School schedulers need to decide whether the benefits of a block schedule seem likely to outweigh the costs associated with the change and whether they have the resources and collective will to support the transition in ways that will foster improved student performance.

Goal 4. Reduce Teaching Load

As discussed previously, one way to improve individual attention for students is to reduce the number of students a teacher sees each week. Reducing the teacher load is accomplished in one of several ways:

a. **Reducing class size.** If a teacher teaches four classes of 20 students, reducing class sizes by 2 would reduce the teaching load by 8, at a tremendous schoolwide cost of about five additional teachers.

b. **Teaching subjects in extended blocks such as a double-length literacy or math class.** Extending blocks reduces the number of distinct classes of students a core teacher sees each week. Double-blocking literacy would thus allow a Fleming teacher to teach only two or three groups of students, reducing teaching load to 40 or 60 students per term.

Double-blocking has the advantage of being a virtually costless way to make a significant reduction in teacher load. In the six-period day, however, the double block replaces the elective period of students. But compare what happens to Fleming teachers as we adopt a six-period, seven-period, or four-block bell schedule (see Figure 8.5). We will assume that class sizes remain at 20 and that teachers retain two planning periods in any of the three scenarios.

In the seven-period and four-block bell schedules, teacher load rises to 100 or up to 120 for noncore teachers, who see five or six groups of students each term, respectively. It drops to 60 for core teachers who each teach three groups of students per day, all year long. Again, for Fleming, none of these schedules costs more than their

Figure 8.5   Teacher load and block scheduling in the Fleming School

Subject	Six-Period Day		Seven-Period Day		4 x 4 or 4 A/B	
	Periods	Teacher Load	Periods	Teacher Load	Periods	Teacher Load
English/ reading	1	80	2	60	2	60
Social studies	1	80	1	100	1	60/120[a]
Math	1	80	1	100	2	60
Science	1	80	1	100	1	60/120[a]
Elective 1	1	80	1	100	1	60/120[a]
Elective 2	1	80	1	100	1	60/120[a]

a. In some block schedules, teachers would see only 60 students per term, but classes would last only part of the year. In other block schedules, noncore teachers would see 120 students per term.

current bell schedule, although success would probably require a professional development investment for literacy or math teachers to work with longer blocked classes.

c. **Teaching in core classes such as humanities or math and science.** Some schools choose to "core" classes by combining English and social studies into a humanities course or combining math and science into one course. This can be done without also implementing extended blocks or in conjunction with extended blocks. Figure 8.6 shows what happens in the three scenarios presented previously if we also combine the double-block math or English with another subject. Pay close attention to what happens to teacher load in the four-block schedule.

What Might Fleming Do?

The authors are tempted to recommend that Fleming adopt the 4 A/B schedule, in which on "A" days, students attend one humanities class that lasts the equivalent of three periods and one elective, and on "B" days, they attend one triple-block math/science class and one other elective. Why? Figure 8.6 shows that the 4 A/B schedule yields a teacher load of 40 for Fleming humanities and math/science teachers, who end up seeing

Figure 8.6 Reducing teacher load by blocking periods in a subject or combining subjects

Subject	Six-Period Day		Seven-Period Day[a]		4 A/B	
	Periods	Teacher Load	Periods	Teacher Load	Periods	Teacher Load
English/ reading	2	40	3	40	3	40
Social Studies	0	N/A	0	N/A	0	N/A
Math	1	80	2	60	3	40
Science	1	80	0	N/A	0	N/A
Elective 1	1	80	1	100	1	60/120[b]
Elective 2	1	80	1	100	1	60/120[b]

a. One triple-block humanities, one double-block math/science, and two electives.
b. In some block schedules, teachers would see only 60 students per term, but classes would last only part of the year. In other block schedules, noncore teachers would see 120 students per term.

two groups of students each. Fleming students spend 75% of their time with two teachers, who get to know them quite well. They also are able to focus virtually all of their time in core academics in long blocks, while still retaining the ability to take two electives classes all year long (although only one on any given day in some schedules). Teams of two core academic teachers are also able to coordinate their schedule to have up to five 80- to 90-minute collaborative planning sessions each week while retaining five extended planning sessions for individual planning. On the other hand, there are a number of tradeoffs to be considered.

Choices and Tradeoffs

We have already pointed out that teaching in longer blocks is not shown to improve student performance alone, although when paired with effective professional development, it seems more likely to have a positive effect. Combining math with science has a more difficult tradeoff because we are essentially trading subject specialization of the teacher for more individual attention for the student. After sixth grade, combining subjects typically requires teachers to be dual certified. In all cases, it is important to make sure that we are not compromising quality of instruction, which consistently proves to be the most important school-controlled factor for improving student performance. Still, the four-block schedule as implemented in Figure 8.6 fosters any number of the strategies we see in high-performing schools: more time in core academics, more individual attention in core academics, and more time for teacher collaboration in longer sessions. It also does not cost any additional money to implement and, in some district situations, would actually free up resources for strategic reallocation.

Goal 5. Vary Time Based on Student Need

The fifth and final goal we set for the Fleming School schedule was to help us vary time based on the needs of students and student groups. There are many options available to us. High-performing schools might accomplish this by

- **Varying length of classes based on student need.** In the Fleming example, we could double-block math only for students not meeting math standards. Or, if we defined sixth grade as a priority year, we could require all Fleming sixth-graders to adopt an academics-focused schedule.
- **Requiring some students to take extra core academic courses.** With or without blocking courses, we could simply require students not meeting standards to take additional core academic classes.
- **Varying the daily start or dismissal time based on student need.** Earlier, we presented the case of the Tech Boston Academy, which extended the school day for all students but allowed some students to earn the right to leave early. Essentially, they lengthened the school day for struggling students.
- **Providing summer or extended-learning opportunities for struggling students.** When students are multiple years behind grade-level standards, it is nearly impossible for them to catch up to their peers without a significant investment that may include summer school or other extended-learning programs.

What Might Fleming Do?

In this case, if Fleming adopted the four-block schedule, all Fleming students would end up spending a significant amount of time (75%) in core academics. Also, because teacher load would be cut in half, we could increase the teachers' ability to use formative assessments to customize lesson plans so they can meet the individual needs of students, probably without making any additional adjustments to the schedule. If the Fleming School did not choose a four-block schedule, we would probably recommend a seven-period schedule and suggest Fleming require a double-block of math or literacy for students not meeting standards. For students who needed even more time than provided by the block schedule or extra classes, we might also recommend an extended-learning or summer program. Of course, there are many other excellent options. As usual, any decision we make will entail tradeoffs.

Choices and Tradeoffs

Research supports the idea that continually assessing student needs is one of the most leveraged ways for a struggling school to improve the performance of its students. It is no coincidence, then, that we think lowering teacher loads from 150 (which we see regularly in urban districts) to 40 or 50 is something that will have a tremendous potential impact on student performance. In this case, the four-block schedule we would recommend does not require schools to vary time by students because in the Fleming School, we think it appropriate that all students focus heavily on core academics. There are many communities and schools where such a heavy focus would not necessarily be appropriate.

STEP 5: CREATE A STRATEGY BY CHOOSING A SET OF OPTIONS THAT WORKS FOR YOU

In discussing the Fleming example, our hope has been to capture and reflect the thoughts and ideas of the dynamic principals whose scheduling lessons and collective wisdom we are attempting to share. In that spirit, we would also like to share a few selection considerations for determining when to adopt the five scheduling goals we highlighted in this chapter (see Figure 8.7).

Clearly, this list of five goals and selection considerations is not meant to be exhaustive. We do hope that it is a useful list that conveys the spirit with which principals of high-performing schools approach the scheduling process. By now it should be clear that schedules have many different purposes and priorities that must be considered together. In some contexts, for instance, a high percentage of time dedicated to English and math might represent a clear strategic focus. In other contexts, it might not be as appropriate. The key is to clearly define scheduling goals that will help students (and adults) develop the desired skills, knowledge, and character and then

Figure 8.7   Crafting a schedule: Summary selection considerations

Typical Strategy	Selection Considerations	Strategic Fit When . . .
Increase common planning time.	Is vital to improvement but is also easy to implement disastrously in absence of expert content support (e.g., coaches) and a clear set of goals, objectives, key activities, and rubrics.	Expert content support is available; formative assessments are in place; there is no common planning time built into the schedule yet; some teacher teams are struggling.
Increase overall instruction time.	Are students behind grade level in core academic subjects? Does the school schedule have a lot of maintenance or support and enrichment activities during the school day? Is the school day short?	Students are behind and unlikely to catch up in time currently available; opportunities exist to reallocate existing time toward instruction; money exists to lengthen the school day.
Increase time in English/ language arts (ELA) and math (or core academics generally).	Are your graduate requirements tougher than mandated by state or district? Does your existing schedule already allot more time to subjects of highest priority? Do struggling students spend 40% or less of instructional time in ELA and math?	Many students are behind in basic literacy or numeracy; the schedule does not prioritize literacy and math or core academics; teaching quality investments are not undercut by increases in academic time.
Reduce teacher load.	Are your teacher loads in core academic subjects more than 70? 140? Are teachers given time to constantly adjust lesson plans to meet individual needs? Do teachers have time to respond meaningfully to challenging homework assignments for all students?	Teacher loads in core academic subjects are higher than 70; you (and faculty) are willing to consider block scheduling or combining subjects; teachers do not have enough time to thoroughly respond to and mark up student assignments (especially writing).
Vary time based on needs.	Do you have a wide range of student academic needs? Do all student schedules look roughly similar? Do you have supports in place to help teachers assess needs accurately and continuously?	Student schedules do not vary based on need; teachers have means to assess need of individual students.

to craft a schedule that accomplishes those goals. An effective schedule can become a core part of the identity of a school and can be a source of pride as well as a key component of success. Creating a successful process for evaluating and refining your schedule can be more important than the process for crafting it in the first place. In the next chapter, we turn to the critical question of how to implement a professional development strategy that works with your chosen schedule.

How to Strategically Improve Teaching Quality

9

We turn now to discussing more of the nuts and bolts of creating a strategic plan to continuously improve the quality of teaching. In Chapter 3, we proposed that strategic schools: (a) hire new teachers and assign them to teacher teams in accordance with a clear plan, (b) adopt well-designed models of job-embedded professional development for existing faculty, (c) create blocks of time for teachers to collaborate, and (d) promote the individual career development of faculty and staff members. We discussed strategies for creating collaborative time in the scheduling chapter, so this chapter will focus on the other three components of a strategic plan for improving the quality of instruction.

Each chapter in this implementation section covers a different strategic planning topic. Readers should begin Part III by reading Chapter 6, because it introduces the Fleming case example, including an assessment of Fleming's academic needs. Chapters 7 through 9 can be read in any order. They follow the same basic process for creating a strategic plan:

1. Determine your school's highest-priority academic needs.

2. Assess how well your resources are aligned with your academic needs.

3. Set concrete goals that meet your highest-priority needs.

4. Identify and evaluate actions for accomplishing your goals.

5. Create a strategy by choosing a set of actions that works for you.

We discuss implementation and measurement of progress in Chapter 10, "Putting It All Together."

STEP 1: DETERMINE YOUR SCHOOL'S HIGHEST-PRIORITY ACADEMIC NEEDS

Recall from Chapter 6 that we summarized the pressing academic needs of Fleming students as follows:

- Math scores started low and declined the longer students stayed in school.
- Critical thinking and problem solving were weak across the curriculum.
- English/language arts (ELA) student performance did not meet school goals.
- There were no discernible performance differences among the more than 90% of students who were Hispanic or African American based on ethnicity.
- Student performance in the areas of math, English, and critical thinking were uniformly low; there were no students at advanced levels, and few students scored proficient.

Fleming's principal also discovered as she reviewed her student performance data that third-grade math scores were particularly low. Based on this finding, she designated third-grade math as a high-priority area and decided to evaluate the capacities of the third-grade teacher team.

STEP 2: ASSESS HOW WELL YOUR RESOURCES ARE ALIGNED WITH YOUR ACADEMIC NEEDS

In Chapter 6, we presented two tools to help assess resource alignment: the Strategic School Resource Diagnostic Tool and the Fleming Teacher Inventory. Principles A to D of the Strategic School Resource Diagnostic Tool (pages 109–112) present a set of questions for evaluating opportunities to strengthen your school's efforts to improve the quality of teaching:

- Does your school use a strategic, rigorous screening and hiring process that includes protocol questions, rubrics, and other ways to evaluate the overall fit and philosophy of potential job candidates?
- Are teacher teams created thoughtfully to ensure that experience and expertise are targeted to high-need areas and that all teams have the support they need?
- Does your school have an individual plan for the development of all teachers, especially new teachers, and do you provide systematic leadership and promotion opportunities for aspiring teacher leaders?

Consider how Fleming would respond to these questions. Because Fleming has no plan for strategic teacher hiring, has no collaborative planning time, and has not adopted a model for providing expert support to help teachers improve their practice, they would answer no to all of these questions. Moreover, the school itself offered no systematic support for teachers to develop individual capacity or reward exceptional performance, including new teachers.

While this initial examination of support for teaching quality suggests that the school's resource allocation does not support improved teaching quality, a close examination of the school's responses to the Teacher Inventory (see Figure 6.6) sheds more light on teaching needs specific to the school. For example, considering that third-grade math performance was particularly problematic, examine the third-grade teaching team to search for insight into the problem. The Fleming Teacher Inventory shows the following regarding the third-grade team:

- No teacher had fully implemented the school's new math program in his or her classroom.
- No teacher had more than five years of experience.
- Three teachers were rated at the novice level, and one was rated at the next level—journeyman—but none were rated to be a practitioner or an expert.
- One third-grade teacher, Harris, who had two years of experience, had not yet implemented the new math program in her classroom. She also had especially low student performance, and the team leader, Stewart, also had low student performance and low levels of implementation of the new curriculum.

The first-grade team inventory contrasts sharply with this picture. The teachers in all four first-grade classrooms implemented the new math program at high levels, and all exceeded student performance expectations. In addition, three of the four teachers possessed the highest teacher proficiency rating in this rubric, "expert." These findings suggest that the Fleming School is not aligning its most expert teachers with its most pressing student needs.

If you have not already done so, we invite you to pause to download the Strategic School Resource Diagnostic Tool or Teacher Inventory from www.educationresourcestrategies.org and complete the tools using your own school's data. As you complete these exercises, ask yourself how well your professional development investments are meeting your school's academic needs.

STEP 3: SET CONCRETE GOALS THAT MEET YOUR TEACHING QUALITY NEEDS

The next step involves setting goals. Your own goals will depend on where you are as a school, including your needs, priorities, and philosophies. Figure 9.1 illustrates how the needs and capacities of both students and teachers affect the types of goals that schools might want to set related to improving teaching quality.

If your school falls in the upper right-hand quadrant of Figure 9.1 with a strong teaching staff and student performance, you are in the luxurious position of being able to consider ways to improve teacher collaboration, nurture teacher leaders from within your own staff, and refine systems for the individual career growth of faculty and staff. You will still want to make sure you have a long-range hiring plan to ensure the continuation of your success.

On the other hand, if you have low teacher capacity and low student performance, you will need to find outside resources to provide expert support. You should seek out a professional development protocol or model that is specific to your challenges. You need to focus on hiring new individuals who can bring deeper skills to your staff and on identifying individual teachers who are having special trouble. It is important to use your system's evaluation process to clearly explain expectations and performance standards, the consequences of continued poor performance, and the supports provided to help teachers improve.

Again referring to the Fleming Teacher Inventory, we see that teaching capacity at the school is mixed, with both experienced teachers and relatively new teachers. More important than experience, teacher proficiency as represented by the evaluation ratings shows that Fleming has some experts but a slightly higher concentration at the lowest two levels of novice or journeyman. Finally, as we discussed,

Figure 9.1 Potential areas of emphasis depending on capacity and student performance needs

		Low	High
Student Performance	*High*	• Emphasize finding resources for expert support. • Use highly specified protocols/models for PD.	• Emphasize teacher assignment. • Nurture teacher leaders for ongoing PD. • Refine systems for individual growth.
	Low	• Hire strategically for open positions. • Use individual teacher evaluations to determine employment status and support needed.	• Use expert resources to work with teacher leaders. • PD focus on teacher-identified challenges.
		Low	*High*
		Teacher Capacity	

NOTE: PD = professional development.

student performance is unacceptably low. This quick evaluation suggests that Fleming falls in the lower left quadrant, with a few instances where it could use strategies from the lower right quadrant for teachers with higher capacity.

What Might Fleming Do?

The Fleming School has many and varied challenges with its student performance and teaching staff. It is nearly impossible to tackle all problems at the same time. The Fleming School might want to focus its immediate efforts on three primary areas:

- **Systematically improve the capacity and fit of new teacher hires** so that teaching quality will improve over time and all new teachers will be willing to implement the school's chosen approach and curriculum.
- **Create collaborative teams of teachers** who meet regularly to discuss assessments of student performance and other student work and to adjust instruction to ensure that all students meet

standards and that all teams have the support needed to collaborate effectively.

- **Develop an effective model for expert support** for all teachers that focuses in particular on the high-need area of math.

If you have not already set specific goals for your own school for improving the quality of teaching, take a moment to do so now. Once your goals are set, the next step is to consider various actions to address each goal.

STEP 4: IDENTIFY AND EVALUATE OPTIONS FOR ACCOMPLISHING YOUR GOALS

Since everything revolves around the quality of teaching and how well teachers work together to adjust instruction in response to student need, most schools will adopt goals that look very similar to the Fleming goals. They may differ in emphasis and certainly specifics of implementation, and that is what we discuss here (see Figure 9.2).

Goal 1. Improve the Capacity and Fit of New Teacher Hires

Most school leaders agree that choosing the right staff and using them most effectively is their most important job. Strategic school leaders begin the process by creating a profile of their faculty and staff. They create a hiring and staffing strategy by

a. Developing a long-range hiring plan

b. Establishing a rigorous hiring process around criteria that meet school needs

c. Using each vacancy as an opportunity to strengthen and evaluate their school organization

a. Develop a long-range hiring plan. How does a school create a detailed, long-range hiring plan? The first step is to understand how well or poorly your current staff capabilities match your instructional vision. This allows you to systematically create the organization required to support your vision. Suppose, for instance, that a school leader wanted to eliminate pull-out instruction for ELL during the day and incorporate all support into the regular classroom. In that school, virtually all new hires would need to be trained and certified to work with ELL students. They

Figure 9.2   Three goals for improving teaching quality and strategies for meeting them

Common Teaching Quality Goal	Options for Action
Goal 1: Improve the capacity and fit of new teacher hires.	• Create a long-term hiring plan. • Establish a hiring process and criteria. • Use each vacancy to strengthen the school organization.
Goal 2: Create collaborative teacher teams, and ensure that each team works.	• Implement collaborative planning time for review of student work. • Define teacher teams and assign responsibilities. • Develop a yearlong schedule for common and PD time.
Goal 3: Develop an effective model for expert support.	• Decide on a PD delivery method. • Define responsibilities and requisite skills of PD provider or coach. • Recruit, find, and screen PD providers.

NOTE: PD = professional development.

would also need to be committed to serving these students in regular-education environments.

A long-range hiring plan should build from the leader's instructional vision to sketch out

- the number and type of classroom teachers needed in each subject and grade with which certifications, skills, or training interests;
- the kinds of expert resources needed for leading teacher teams and building teacher skills in certain subject areas;
- the kinds of subject specialists necessary to provide individualized instruction in reading and math; and
- the schedules teachers will need to work and whether the workday needs to differ by type of teacher.

Knowing the answers to these questions also informs the process needed to locate teachers who meet these more clearly-defined needs. These answers help school leaders use a more targeted recruiting strategy and a more rigorous hiring process.

b. Establish a hiring process built around criteria that meet your school's needs. Principals in high-performing schools use the hiring process to choose teachers who will fit the school's instructional design. They take pains to set expectations clearly about what will be expected of teachers in their school. They write clear job descriptions and establish rubrics for evaluating each candidate's fit for the open position. They consider whether an applicant's skills and experiences complement those of other members of the team he or she will be joining. They also evaluate whether the teacher's philosophy and disposition will mesh with the philosophy and learning community in the school.

For instance, Deborah Meir (1992), the founder of Central Park East, a high school in New York City, described five qualities she looks for in prospective teachers:

- self-conscious reflectiveness about how they themselves learn and maybe even more, how and when they do not learn;
- a sympathy toward others, an appreciation of their differences, an ability to imagine their "otherness";
- a willingness to engage in, or better yet a taste for, collaborative work;
- a desire to have others to share some of one's own interests; and
- perseverance, energy, and devotion to getting things right.

These criteria are reminiscent of those proposed by the National Board for Professional Teaching Standards, that all teachers have: a commitment to students and learning, an ability to think systematically about their practice and learn from experience, and the desire and skill set to work together with other teachers as "members of learning communities" (www.nbpts.org/the_standards).

c. Use each vacancy as an opportunity to strengthen and evaluate your organization. Every vacancy provides a chance to re-examine the school organization. Are there individuals already working in the school who might benefit from adopting a new role, learning a new subject area, or working with different grade levels or teacher teams? Does adding a new teacher into a team change the group dynamics? Might it prompt other personnel moves? Is there an opportunity to rewrite a standard job description provided by the school system? Noted Boston Principal Mary Nash asserts:

> The hiring process is the first time we make our expectations for teachers clear. We try to communicate the demanding nature of the work we do in this school, the multiple responsibilities

teachers have, as well as the kind of commitment and teamwork we expect. Working here is not for everyone, but those who choose it become part of a truly unique school community that is getting better at improving instruction every day.

The vacancies also offer an opportunity to move teachers to different grades or subjects depending on certifications. Done purposefully, this could fill a gap in experience across a grade-level team, provide support to a different group of teachers, or give teachers an opportunity to learn new grade-level content and strategies. Many teachers find it rewarding to expand their experience, especially when it comes with leadership opportunities that enable them to make more of a difference for students by helping other teachers.

Depending on your district context, you may feel you have limited control over hiring. You may rely on the district to send you candidates and may have to work with a committee to select teachers. You may be required to choose the most senior teacher even if you feel he or she may not be the most qualified or the best fit with the chemistry of your staff. These are clearly real constraints. What we can say is that if you don't have a clear plan for what you are looking for and what it means to be a teacher in your school that you can communicate to potential transfers or new hires, then you don't have a chance of influencing things in your direction. We have conducted hundreds of interviews with principals who work in districts where the constraints look much like the ones listed here, and we can tell you that these principals do exert significant control over which new teachers come into their building. They do this by always being on the lookout for good new teachers, having a pool of substitutes who work regularly in the building, and taking teachers on provisional status. They work through the interview process to discourage candidates they don't want and encourage those they do.

What Might Fleming Do?

Hiring needs to be a priority at the Fleming given the relatively low teacher capacity; the long history of teachers working independently; the reluctance to implement district and instructional strategies; and pressing student performance needs in ELA, special education, math, and literacy. In earlier chapters, we suggested that Fleming implement flexible grouping strategies to bring more individual attention into classrooms around ELA and math. The Fleming leadership will need to seriously assess whether all of the teachers in the school have the capacity and commitment to implement a schoolwide program and to collaborate in new ways to do so. To use resources more effectively across programs to provide individual attention, Fleming needs to recruit teachers who have content skills as well as bilingual or special-education certification.

Choices and Tradeoffs

Making sure that each new hire fits school needs is always a good idea. However, figuring out how much to invest to build the skills or change the attitudes of existing staff versus finding new teachers who might infuse needed expertise and energy is one of the most difficult choices school leaders face. Too often, leaders get little help from school systems in facing it. Investing to support one low-performing individual teacher diverts energy from other critical tasks like building a collaborative teaching staff. Similarly, taking the time and following all the requirements to formally document low performance and facilitate teacher replacement can be onerous. School leaders face a difficult tradeoff, especially when the school confronts pressing performance challenges overall. Should leaders focus time to build the skills of low performers, work to replace the teacher, or leave that aside and focus on building skills of those willing and able?

We have no neat framework to solve this dilemma—but we offer a couple of observations to consider when weighing the tradeoffs. First, principals tell us and research confirms that they are good at identifying the least-effective teachers and the best teachers but are not as good at distinguishing talent in the middle (Jacob & Lefgren, 2006). Second, there is some evidence that the lowest-performing teachers stay low performing even with intervention (Weerasinghe & Anderson, 2001). Third, as we have discussed, improving schoolwide performance takes everyone in the school—one year with a poor teacher can set performance back significantly (Rivkin, Hanushek, & Kain, 2002; Weerasinghe & Anderson, 2001).

Goal 2. Create Collaborative Teacher Teams and Ensure That Each Team Works

Strategic schools build collaborative teacher teams by

a. defining teacher teams and assigning responsibilities, and

b. developing yearlong schedules for common and professional development time.

a. Define teacher teams and assign responsibilities. Creating the school schedule and designing professional development requires that school leaders have a clear sense of which teachers share work and what activities or learning teacher teams should be working on. Real teamwork requires that team members share common work and each have a stake in the effective outcome of this work. In traditional elementary schools, four main combinations of teachers share common work—grade-level homeroom teachers, grade-level and specialist teachers, content area across the grade span, and schoolwide teachers. Grade-level homeroom teachers—for example, first-grade teachers—have the most intensive need for regular collaboration. These teachers share the same student learning goals, the same curriculum materials, and in many cases, the same units and daily lessons. Although they usually do not share the same students, they struggle with the common challenges of mapping curriculum to standards, learning new curriculum and content material, planning lessons, and assessing student progress.

Grade-level teachers also need to coordinate and, in some cases, work closely with specialist teachers who share their students—most important, those who provide specialized support for students, including those in special-education, gifted, and bilingual programs. Too often, teachers do not have regular time to work with specialists who serve their students to ensure integration of instruction, and worse, there is little expectation that they do so. Teachers share common work across grade levels as well, because they have collective responsibility for student learning over time, and the curriculum material from one year must link to the next. This work of clarifying expectations for learning and developing a coherent curriculum and instructional approach over time should happen by content area, and time and leadership should be devoted to it. Schoolwide, teachers also share work on instruction-related activities such as schoolwide theme days, discipline, and promotion policies.

Subject specialization at the secondary school level makes defining the primary teacher team more difficult. Secondary schools face a fundamental tradeoff between collaborating to improve instructional content in subject areas or coming together around shared students. The popular design structure of breaking schools into "clusters" or "houses" places the emphasis on sharing students. In this model, a group of students share the same set of core academic teachers, who work as a team to coordinate instruction across subjects and keep track of individual student progress. Shared teacher time is often scheduled by cluster, with collaboration around content-area instruction happening during other time slots, if at all. The traditional high school department structure focuses on collaboration around improving instruction by subject area. In this model, teachers do not share students but they teach students the same material, so they can jointly devise lessons, compare results, and test improved instruction.

Clearly, it makes sense for teachers to collaborate around *both* shared students and instructional challenges. Many school leaders have partially addressed this by focusing on improving the instruction of writing and having all teachers, regardless of subject, set common student learning goals, learn common instructional techniques, and use common assessment tools. But this kind of collaboration cannot take the place of work to improve more specific subject-area learning goals and lessons. The relative emphasis (shared students vs. shared content) depends on the school design, student performance priorities, and teacher capacity. Study after study shows that professional development around the actual instructional goals and material has the most direct impact on improving instruction (Cohen & Hill, 2000; Elmore, 2002). This means that in cases of low student performance or teacher capacity, the first priority for collaboration should be around content and how to teach it.

Leaders of small secondary schools face a particular challenge in finding ways to help teachers work together to improve content-area instruction (Education Resource Strategies & Annenberg Institute, 2004). In a larger secondary school, as many as three to five math teachers might share the same grade, learning goals, and curriculum materials. However, a small high school may have only one or two teachers who teach tenth-grade math. Leaders of these smaller schools must plan other ways to support continuous improvement of content area instruction using coaches, cross-school collaboration, and other professional development resources at the district level or through online or professional networks.

Clarity around who should be meeting and what teachers should be doing informs the scheduling of time, assignment of teachers to groups, and support that might be needed. Figure 9.3 defines four categories of instructional activities that teacher teams spend time working together on. What teachers should work on depends on teacher expertise and school context—especially whether it is a start-up and part of a system of schools. In new, standalone schools, it may make sense for teachers to spend time defining learning and performance standards, choosing assessment tools, and developing curriculum frameworks. Too often, teacher teams devote too much time to activities that others could do more effectively for them. For example, we have worked with many teacher teams that spend most of their precious time organizing student performance data and trying to graph it in useful ways—rather than working with useful, detailed reports to determine how to improve instruction. School leaders can maximize the impact of teacher time by providing support that allows teachers to focus on the activities they are most expert on and that are closest to classroom instruction—marked by the Xs in the boxes in Figure 9.3.

Figure 9.3 Focus of teacher time

Instructional Activity	Focus of Teacher Time	Support Needed
Defining student performance standards		• Standards defined to actionable level
Aligning curriculum with standards by subject and grade		• Powerful curriculum material • Aligned curriculum frameworks • Literacy models

Aligning instructional strategies with standards:
  1. Lesson plans
  2. Classroom assignments
  3. Grouping strategies
  4. Use of instructional time
	XXXX	• Literacy models
		• Instructional coaching
		• Powerful curriculum materials
		• Training in content
		• Coaching feedback

Using ongoing measurement of student progress to monitor instructional effectiveness	XX	• Assessment tools • Timely analysis and presentation of student performance data in useful formats • Instructional management tools

b. Develop yearlong schedule for common and professional development time. School leaders must define the members of each teacher team, their key collaborative goals, and the duration and frequency of time needed before creating a master schedule and yearly professional development calendar. To support this effort, the leadership team might complete a table like the one in Figure 9.4. With such a calendar, common planning time can be scheduled, the use of professional development days can be plotted, and additional time can be scheduled when substitutes are used to cover teacher times or stipends are used for afterschool time.

What Might Fleming Do?

The Fleming may want to use findings from its Teacher Inventory to reassign teachers to different grades to create effective collaborative teacher teams. For example, the principal may want to exchange an expert first-grade teacher—one of three strong teachers in this grade—with a third-grade teacher with less experience. Such a change would bring expertise to another grade and team, provide additional support to

Figure 9.4   Example: Calendar to ensure teacher team time is used strategically

Teacher Team	Focus of Team Effort	How Much Time	How Often	Support Needed
Grade 1	Reading comprehension	90 minutes	Weekly	ELA coach
Grade 2	Complex problem solving	90 minutes	Weekly	Grade-level team leader
Grade 3	Writing	90 minutes	Weekly	ELA coach
Subject area team leaders	Transitions between grades	2 hours	Monthly	Principal
Teachers schoolwide	Readers Workshop	4 hours	Bimonthly	ELA coach
Instructional leadership team		2 hours	Biweekly	Principal; alternating ELA coach/ math coach
New teachers		4 hours	Weekly	Mentor/coach
Teachers in need of improvement		6 hours	Weekly	Principal/ coach

NOTE: ELA = English/language arts.

struggling teachers, and give accomplished teachers a leadership opportunity in the school.

Second, the school will need to create time for teams to work together. At the Fleming School, we would suggest that meeting in grade-level teams is a top priority to ensure uniformly high levels of implementation of the school's chosen math and literacy programs. Furthermore, with restructured teams, this will leverage existing expertise.

Choices and Tradeoffs

There are two sets of choices and tradeoffs associated with this goal of creating collaborative teams. First, reassigning teachers to new grade levels or subjects and moving teachers from teaching one grade to another requires that these teachers learn new subject matter and can cause short-term disruption. On the other hand, when implemented as part of a strategy to leverage teacher expertise, it can be viewed as an exciting opportunity for the individuals involved.

Second, especially at the middle-school level, leaders face a choice about how to structure their teacher teams and focus their use of time. As we discussed previously, grouping teachers in teams that share students allows them to talk about common learning issues across courses and to work on the teaching of shared content such as writing. However, grouping teachers who share exactly the same content and student performance goals allows much more focused collaboration and professional development. In the case of low performance and capacity, we would argue that shared content should be the priority teaming goal.

Goal 3. Develop a Model for Providing Expert Support to Improve Instruction

Our research and experience suggests three strategies for designing and implementing well-designed professional development. These components are as follows:

    a. Adopt or devise an appropriate professional development delivery method.

    b. Define responsibilities and required expertise of professional development staff.

    c. Recruit, find, and screen professional developers or coaches.

a. Adopt or devise an appropriate professional development delivery method to meet the priority. Because each school has different needs and capacities, there is no one professional development delivery model that will always be most appropriate. Multiple approaches should be considered. For instance, a school where teachers are just learning to work together to use assessments of student work to adjust instruction might benefit from using the Standards in Practice Model described in Chapter 3 to create a common language, protocol, and focus for its work. However, schools with high levels of expertise and a clearly defined curriculum might choose the Lesson Study method (also detailed in Chapter 3) as a way to promote collaboration and continuous improvement.

b. Define responsibilities and required skills of professional development staff. As described in Chapter 3, coaching is an essential component to effective professional development. However, simply hiring a coach and leaving him or her to "go for it" is not enough. Too often, districts and schools provide coaching support without clearly defining what priorities they expect coaches to address, the plan for how they will work in schools, and the skills and dispositions they will need to meet these needs. As discussed previously, a school whose professionals are just beginning to organize into teams with a new principal will need a different mix of expertise than one with a highly experienced instructional leader as principal who has already launched the first phases of improvement and is delving deeply into how to improve content area instruction. Similarly, a school that already has highly expert teacher leaders who can serve as coaches will need to organize in different ways.

The planned model for coaching also affects the job definition and selection process. If coaches are expected to work with instructional teams during common planning time scheduled throughout the week, provide individual classroom support in targeted classrooms, and facilitate a weekly schoolwide professional development time slot, this obviously has implications for when the hired coach needs to be available. Although this need to match coaching availability to the professional development time available sounds obvious, we often find schools who have hired coaches or assigned teacher leaders without creating formally scheduled times to work with teachers and so find themselves constantly idle or "forcing" themselves on teachers. The outside coach might be assigned to come once every couple of weeks without a scheduled time—matching no team's particular schedule and no specific plan for which teachers need support.

Your school's definition of coaching and teacher leadership responsibilities should fit your own priorities and skill needs. Again, refer to the Strategic School Resource Diagnostic Tool, Principle B (page 110), to re-examine whether you have already aligned coaching to staff need. This definition might include a high-level definition of coaches' expected role, a listing of responsibilities, and a clear definition of skills, experiences, and characteristics required. Deanna Burney has created a generic coaching job description that defines what successful instructional support and content coaches should be able to do (Education Resource Strategies & Annenberg Institute, 2004). She states that such coaches must be able to interpret data on student performance and analyze classroom assignments to identify areas for instructional improvement. But just as important, she highlights the systemic thinking and communication skills that would enable coaches to ensure that the work they do with individual teachers links to the larger implications for the school and grade-level team as a whole. The Boston Plan for Excellence, which hired and helped support the first instructional coaches used in Boston, created a concrete list of coaching responsibilities included in the coaching contract that specified that coaches must guide schools through completing the district's "Whole School Improvement Essentials" and plan a transition process, in which external coaching would no longer be needed by

- Setting a schedule for the year's work
- Developing a flexible, integrated budget for the use of professional development–related funds
- Facilitating ongoing working sessions of instructional leadership and instructional teams
- Highlighting areas for additional expert assistance or support
- Identifying needed tools, staff development, or support materials
- Facilitating teacher teams that meet regularly to look at student work in relation to the Boston Public Schools (BPS) Citywide Learning Standards
- Assisting schools to complete the following requirements:
  o Implementing an instructional focus
  o Looking at student work in relation to the BPS Citywide Learning Standards to identify students' needs, improve instruction, assess students, and inform professional development
  o Making hard choices about current resources to best support the instructional focus
  o Setting benchmarks for student improvement and developing an internal accountability system that is linked to the BPS accountability system
  o Implementing and refining a professional development plan (Boston Plan for Excellence, 2002)

Boston coaching responsibilities also included participating in and contributing to a districtwide network of coaches and communicating progress toward school-level targets and professional development plans.

The previous job descriptions fit a coach who would be initiating a whole-school change effort. A school needing a literacy or math coach would need to screen coaches for different knowledge, as would a school focusing on integrating special-education students more effectively into regular classrooms.

c. Recruit, find, and screen professional developers or coaches. Expert teachers do not always make excellent coaches, and finding individuals who can play this role can be challenging. Even though applicants may be well known or respected in a school or have specific status as a "lead teacher" or National Board Certification, they may not have the right combination of skills and experiences to be a powerful coach. The decision of whether to use an "internal" coach—one who is part of the school staff—or an "external" coach who comes from the outside depends on the characteristics of the potential coach as well as the teachers' willingness to open their practice to critique. Sometimes, teachers who have worked in a school for many years find it difficult to critique and provide guidance for teachers they have known for so long. Also, it can be hard for teachers to view a long-known colleague as an "expert" who views their work with all its difficulty and opportunity for improvement. This can be especially difficult if teachers resist the introduction of new strategies or are just learning to open their practice to professional critique and collaboration.

All coaching candidates, whether internal or external, should "apply" for the position and be carefully screened using a combination of carefully crafted interviews along with observation to determine their skills. Deanna Burney describes a screening process that asks coach candidates to (Education Resource Strategies & Annenberg Institute, 2004)

- Explain how he or she would respond to a concrete problem grounded in instructional practice, and explain how the candidate would identify, collect, and use data to solve the problem, including how he or she would discuss findings with the teacher orally and in writing. Burney says that interviewers should look for the ability to develop multiple solutions to solving the problem, use multiple forms of evidence to verify conclusions, and communicate one's ideas with teachers effectively and professionally, both orally and in writing.
- Provide a video of his or her teaching practice, or teach a lesson in the subject area of his or her specialty.
- Interpret data presented in various formats, including student work samples, and its implications for classroom practice.
- Complete tasks collaboratively to ensure that coaching candidates feel comfortable with "give and take" between peers.

You may find that none of your existing teachers, even those who act as lead teachers, yet have the skills required to be excellent instructional coaches. However, it may be possible to develop their leadership potential by pairing them with an external coach for a period of time. Even though it may seem to make sense—and certainly feels easier in the short run—to hire an internal coach, teachers who make the best coaches don't always stay working in schools. Many can be found in university settings or working as consultants outside of school systems.

Many schools work in districts where the district runs the coaching program and specifies the model of coaching. In these cases, the coach may be hired and assigned to schools with little input from the schools about what expertise, attitudes, and responsibilities they need. If this is true, you will need to proactively manage this process by being clear and firm about your priorities and needs. We have worked with many a principal who refused the district coaching resource rather than introduce an ill-qualified, misaligned distraction into their school. Other principals have chosen to work closely with the coach to maximize the benefit, and they provide concrete feedback to the district if the coach truly did not support teachers in improving instruction.

What Might Fleming Do?

Fleming needs to develop a strategic and purposeful strategy for bringing in expert support. Because the needs and experience of Fleming staff are diverse and the teaching teams are beginning to work together in new ways, it is best to hire such a person from outside the school to provide ongoing support and an impartial perspective. The leadership team of the school should create a specific job description that requires expertise in coaching math—the students' high-need area—and experience coaching reluctant teachers.

Choices and Tradeoffs

As discussed previously, the primary choice when selecting a model for expert support is whether to invest in outside expertise versus finding ways to leverage internal expertise in combination with more targeted use of external experts. Again, in situations of low capacity or stagnant student performance, outside expertise can infuse new energy and ideas. Research consistently confirms that schools that make dramatic improvement do invest in outside experts (Education Trust, 1999; Odden et al., 2006).

STEP 5: CREATE A STRATEGY BY CHOOSING A SET OF OPTIONS THAT WORKS FOR YOU

As you explore the Fleming example, we hope that you have noticed the similarities and differences between this example and your own school. As we noted, all schools should have similar high-level goals for improving teaching quality—the differences will be in the emphasis you place on certain components of your strategy and in the way you organize and structure your teaching teams, collaborative time, and professional development (see Figure 9.5).

Figure 9.5   Summary selection considerations for strategically improving teaching quality

Typical Strategy	Selection Considerations	Strategic Fit When . . .
Improve the capacity and fit of new teacher hires.	• Do you already have a long-range hiring plan and process that includes written job descriptions and a process to ensure that your staffing structures and assignments evolve to meet student needs? • Districts and unions may command a powerful voice in determining what teachers are assigned to what schools. Principals will need to be deliberate and persistent to hire the staff they want.	• You do not have a concrete and purposeful hiring plan. • You have a significant mismatch between the teaching expertise you need and what you have. • You anticipate staff vacancies.
Create collaborative teacher teams and ensure that each team works.	• Do you have a concentration of novice teachers in certain subjects and grades? • Do you have a balance of teacher qualifications across subjects and grades? • Are your most expert teachers assigned to meet your highest student performance priorities? • Have you organized teachers in teams that allow sharing of different skills and expertise? • Working together as a team can be a new experience for some teachers and may need significant support as the work progresses.	• Your staff has a high proportion of new teachers or overall low capacity. • Your expertise is not spread evenly across the school. • You hire a coach who can facilitate these teams and make sure they are effective. Or • You have a high level of teacher expertise, but teachers do not collaborate to improve instruction schoolwide.
Develop an effective model for expert support.	• Do you use outside coaches or internal expertise to support improved teaching? • Do you match the expertise of your coaches and lead teachers to the prioritized student and teacher needs? • Coaches can be expensive when used effectively—that is, the coach works with the faculty throughout the year, observing and supporting them both in their classrooms and in small-group debriefs.	• Your staff does not have the capacity to deliver professional development to one another and needs outside support. • The school can access resources to support ongoing, meaningful coaching from external coaches who observe and support teachers in their own classrooms. Or • Internal expertise has not been organized to promote sharing of practice.

In conclusion, when faced with a choice between investing in teaching quality and something else, think hard before investing in something else—even when it means going up against standard practice or conventional wisdom. For example, if reducing class sizes means you will have to take money away from coaching or disrupt teaching teams that are just beginning to work well together, then it is worth taking a second look. Finally, as we have emphasized throughout, the combination of strategies you choose now may not be exactly the right one three years from now, as your student performance needs will change and your teaching capacity will grow.

Putting It
All Together

10

As you worked your way through Chapters 6 through 9, we hope that you were able to gain a clear understanding of your current resource use and have begun designing a strategic plan that leverages all of your resources—people, time, and money—to improve student learning. In this chapter, we discuss the final implementation and monitoring steps: integrating the components into a whole, redeploying resources, and developing the final implementation and monitoring plan.

INTEGRATE THE COMPONENTS OF YOUR PLAN: ENSURE THAT "ALL THE PLANETS ALIGN"

As you explore and decide on the various components of your plan (such as student assignment and grouping, schedule, and a strategy for improving the quality of teaching), it is essential to monitor the compatibility of the different pieces to make sure you do not develop competing strategies and that "all the planets align."

Thus far in the implementation section, we've discussed strategies for assigning faculty and regrouping students, crafting a master schedule that supports your student and faculty priorities, and developing a multiyear plan to systematically improve the quality of teaching. By applying this process to the Fleming School case example, we generated the recommendations summarized in Figure 10.1.

Even if each individual recommendation makes sense, it is important to emphasize that none of these components can be implemented in isolation from the other components. The final choice of a bell schedule will radically affect both the type of professional development needed and the forums in which professional development can be provided. It will also affect the way students are grouped with teachers. Implementing blocked

Figure 10.1   Summary of Fleming recommendations from previous chapters

Organizational Design Component	Current Resource Use at Fleming School	Recommended Changes
Student assignment and grouping strategy	• Yearlong, self-contained classrooms of 20+ students in virtually all grades and subjects.	• Reduce class size (secondary) and group sizes (elementary) in English/language arts and math. • Create teacher teams that share responsibility for groups of students.
Master schedul	• Equal time for all subjects and teachers with same schedule daily. • Teachers had significant nonstudent time but no time set aside for collaboration.	• Craft a schedule that frees up time for teachers to collaborate and that pushes more time to the priority subjects of literacy and math for all students, such as a seven-period or block schedule.
Strategy to improve teaching quality	• Workshops planned yearly as needs arise; individual teacher professional development on request. • No long-range hiring plan.	• Create a multiyear strategy that provides expert support to collaborative teams. • Create a strategic hiring plan.

classes, for instance, might require teachers to learn and embrace new skills and techniques to handle longer sessions. Combining subjects may require teachers to gain additional certifications and content knowledge. Organizing collaboration time requires school leaders to provide expert support and clear guidance on how it is to be used. In some cases and for some students, English/language arts (ELA) teachers might need to learn how to teach reading in addition to literature. Curricula might need to be revised or rewritten. The various components of the strategic design must be considered together and crafted so that each supports the other.

There are several common pitfalls you may want to consider as you tweak the components of your larger strategic plan. First, make sure you take into account the teaching quality implications of your scheduling and grouping decisions. Many structural changes that require expertise or new behaviors from teachers often demand new professional development to help teachers be successful using those new structures. For example, suppose you read the chapter on crafting a master schedule and decided that you wanted to address your students' ELA and math needs by increasing time on core academics and creating a double-block schedule that centers on a 90-minute humanities and math/science block. Then later, as you pored through the chapter "How to Strategically Improve Teaching Quality," you analyzed your Teacher Inventory only to realize that your English teachers are not implementing your new literacy program and hold certification only in that subject. This disconnect—needing teachers to teach two subjects in a longer block while having a staff that is struggling with its current subject—is something that must be reconciled to create an overarching strategic plan that will be successful.

If you do find yourself in this incompatible situation, this doesn't mean you should abandon your plan. You are halfway there, in that at least now you have a vision for where you want to be. While you may not be able to immediately move to create double blocks staffed with skilled teachers, you might take interim steps to getting there. Is there a subset of teachers who have the skills to teach double blocks and could pilot this program with a group of students? Although your English department is not in a position to take on this strategy, what about the math and science department? Could you begin the blocking with those subjects as the English and social studies teachers engage in professional development that would enable them to join in the new schedule next year?

REDEPLOY ALL RESOURCES TO SUPPORT YOUR PLAN

Once you are satisfied with the compatibility of the various components of your strategic plan, you must also determine whether you can afford to implement all of them together and whether there are barriers to implementation. This requires a strategic budgeting process. Most schools approach budgeting as a rote exercise. The new budget is simply the previous budget revised slightly to reflect changes in enrollment and funding levels. The principal finishes the budgeting process by filling any vacancies and then squeezing the tiny pot of discretionary money to fund new curricula and perennial initiatives such as professional development.

For strategic school leaders, in contrast, the budget is the active expression of their strategic leadership. We define strategic school leadership as managing toward a long-range plan that allocates resources to the school's most important priorities in ways most likely to improve student performance.

Strategic School Leadership

Managing toward a long-range plan that allocates resources to the school's most important priorities in ways most likely to improve student performance.

Strategic school leaders define their school's achievement priorities and then translate them into organizational priorities that inform organizational strategies. These organizational strategies sometimes have enormous budget implications. To review all resources and redeploy them in support of your new strategy, you will need to answer three questions:

- Do all existing resources support the new strategy?
- Are there additional ways to leverage expertise inside and outside the school organization?
- Will the new strategy cost additional money or require more teachers?

Do All Existing Resources Support the New Strategy?

Some strategies will require additional resources, while others will not. As a first step in determining whether you can afford your new strategy, it is worthwhile to carefully examine all of the resources in the school to ensure that every dollar and staff person has a clear role that links to the chosen design and vision. Consider the example of the Fleming budget (see Figure 10.2).

School administration totals 7% of the Fleming budget. This includes the principal, assistant principal, and three clerks. The second largest category is student support personnel, including the librarian and the school nurse. For each position, you want to ask the following:

- How necessary is this position, program, or line item to your strategy? (Note that this is a different question than asking whether the position is mandated by district policy or tradition.)
- If it is necessary (or required), is there a way this position might support your instructional vision more fully? For example, should the assistant principal role include less administration and student discipline and more support for teachers individually or during collaborative planning time?
- If you do envision a different role for a position, the next question is: Can *this particular* person play this role? Do you need to provide

Figure 10.2 Fleming school budget (summary level)

Category	Expense	Full-Time Employees	Percentage of Budget
Teachers	$3,078,008	53.0	77%
Instructional aides	$113,012	5.0	3%
Instructional coach	$42,545	0.5	1%
Professional stipends	$5,000		0%
School administration	$262,028	5.0	7%
Substitutes—per diem	$38,603		1%
Librarian	$65,143	1.0	2%
School nurse	$56,928	1.0	1%
Custodian	$115,684	3.0	3%
Food services	$74,288		2%
Instruction textbooks	$41,939		1%
Equipment and supplies	$24,117		1%
Utilities	$52,341		1%
Total	**$3,969,636**	**66.5**	**100%**

professional development or plan to recruit a new individual over time? How does this affect your short-term and long-term hiring plans?

• Can you reduce the cost of these positions by using part-time staff or outsourcing the position to another partner?

Are There Additional Ways to Leverage Expertise Inside and Outside the School Organization?

As you analyze your existing resources and compare them with the resources you need to implement your vision, consider how you can leverage all able bodies—both within and outside the school—to help. Strategic leaders find the lowest-cost way of hiring the expertise needed for their school's organizational design. They invest to leverage the time of their most expert staff by hiring others at lower cost to work with them or investing in equipment that increases their productivity. This can mean contracting out or working with outside partners who can bring needed perspective into the school. To accomplish this, the Graham and Parks School contracted with part-time subject specialists who worked from 10:45 a.m. to 2 p.m. on various days. This solution reduced the cost of providing electives and allowed the creation of a significant block of shared noninstructional time for all teachers. Any solution has tradeoffs, and this one meant that subject specialists could not be part of teacher teams on a regular basis. Given the priorities at Graham and Parks, however, the sacrifice made sense to the leadership team.

The Mary Lyon Elementary School found numerous ways to invest strategically to maximize expertise and instructional resources around its instructional design. As we described earlier, the Mary Lyon School serves a combination of regular-education and intensely needy special-education students in a largely integrated setting with an extended school day. This required very small class sizes with multiple highly-skilled adults. The emotional intensity of the teaching job also required that teachers have significant instruction-free time during the school day. To accomplish these goals using existing resources, Mary Lyon partnered with a local university to provide interns who served as second teachers for every classroom while earning their master's degree. Second, Mary Lyon contracted with outside providers to provide afterschool services and instruction during the school day in subjects such as drama that the existing staff did not have skills or time to cover (Miles & Darling-Hammond, 1997).

The kinds of solutions described here can be difficult to implement in school districts that assign resources to schools as specific staff positions with little left over for discretionary use. However, creative use of both internal and external staff could provide some schools with the flexibility they need to realize their vision.

Will the New Strategy Cost More?

When you created the components of your school's strategic plan, you considered many ideas that would shift teachers to different uses, including some ideas that may require more (or fewer) teachers overall. For instance, you may have decided to redeploy special program and resource teachers to regular classrooms to create individual attention for all students. You might have decided to require that students spend more time in math or ELA. These decisions do not require additional teachers and so are budget neutral, but they do require a shift in staff.

Other staffing changes might require more teachers than currently exist, for instance, a decision to add tutors or itinerant reading teachers to support small-group instruction. Other changes (such as class-size increases) might even free up resources for other priorities. At this point, you need to estimate the budget impact of the desired changes and find ways to free up money to support your new goals.

A common pitfall for principals is a lack of available resources. Often, as principals engage in the process of inventorying and reallocating resources to meet their most pressing needs, they are forced to a halting stop when they add it all up and realize they don't have enough resources to do it all. There are several ways of tackling this problem. First, look at all of your noninstructional spending and staff positions and consider whether you could trade any of those resources for others that impact instruction. The next line of attack is to keep your vision, articulate it clearly to others, and raise outside funds to support it. If that does not work, make tradeoffs. The first place to look for new resources is raising class size—the last choice should be in the area of reducing teaching quality.

IMPLEMENT YOUR PLAN

We feel it is vital to craft a vision for a school that is not constrained by the current barriers and limitations that have resulted from education's structural legacy. However, there is a time to dream and a time to plan. With a vision in mind and a strategy on paper, the next step is to work relentlessly to identify the challenges you face and create a plan to overcome them. This is the work of years. Four implementation steps will help you create a strategic school:

1. Create a plan to overcome implementation barriers.

2. Communicate the new strategy so that the staff and community can share your excitement and own the plan with you.

3. Set measurable indicators of progress and then measure them.

4. Adapt your strategic plan over time, flexibly using resources to support changing situations.

1. Create a Plan to Overcome Implementation Barriers

As you begin to make these final decisions, you will undoubtedly confront challenges to changing the use of staff, time, and money. The most common include funding restrictions, contractual and district policies, and very tough choices.

Funding Restrictions. Although many funding streams like Title I have become much more flexible in recent years, funds still come attached to specific job positions that may or may not make sense given your strategy.

As you develop your strategic plan, we urge you to begin by considering "all money green." By this, we mean that you should figure out how best to reach your goals with the set of resources and *then* find ways to finagle the funding. The first step to addressing funding restrictions is to identify *who* is restricting the use of funds, the district or the funder. Often, central offices create rules and regulations that surround funding streams that help them ensure compliance with the funders' regulation— even though the funder doesn't care that the money be used in exactly that way. A second, related step is to understand the reason the funder specified that funds be used in exactly that way. Then, you can show whether and how your planned use addresses those goals. Finally, if it's important enough, you need to find someone who can help you work it through—as one savvy principal we work with is fond of saying, "Find your friends."

Contractual and District Policies. A host of union and district policies address the definition of the teacher workday, class size, and job responsibilities. Unraveling these would be a worthy topic for a book by itself. We have found that the combined effect of the many possible objections, rules, and regulations to changing the use of resources can stop the process of moving to a new school design before it begins. Many of the existing guidelines, court orders, and contractual stipulations make sense when considered in isolation. For example, it might make sense to mandate that certain students receive additional support outside the regular classroom to meet their needs if the assumption is that teachers in the regular classroom each have 25 students and do not have the skills and knowledge to support these students. But this rule might not be needed in a newly re-envisioned use of resources, in which regular-education classroom teachers have much smaller group sizes for all or part of the day and have the professional development and expert support they need to serve these students well.

It's the *collection* of reasons for not changing existing resource use that get in the way—not any single challenge. Leaders must consider the rules, regulations, and policies in the context of a complete vision for organizing their school to invest in teaching quality, maximize academic time, and ensure individual attention to meet learning priorities. Schools often have difficulty taking the first steps in this process because they don't believe they will be able to implement it. Over and over again, we have found that successful principals suspend disbelief to create a vision worth fighting for. Although they may not reach the vision with the budget they originally submit, they can't argue for it or build toward it if they can't effectively articulate where they want to end up; their budget needs to express their long-term vision.

Tough Choices. In addition to requiring planning, strategic leadership requires making choices—often very difficult ones since a school budget is made primarily of people. Some of these choices will involve eliminating cherished programs that don't align with your school's current instructional priorities. As we have described throughout, strong school leaders evolve much of their organizational plan by creating the strategies with their teaching staff. But in the end, we believe that budget making is not a democratic process. There are some times when school leaders just have to make the tough call to eliminate a position or program because other things are more important.

2. Communicate the New Strategy so That the Staff and Community Can Share Your Excitement and Own the Plan With You

We have never studied a successful strategic school whose faculty was not excited about their school's instructional vision. These schools have gone to great lengths to collaborate with different constituents of the school community to develop, communicate, and implement a strategy that supports teaching and learning.

Faculty buy-in can be achieved in several ways that vary based on teacher leadership structure and formal and informal decision-making processes. Some schools solicit teacher input on strategic plans before making final decisions, while others have teachers on the team making the actual decisions. In many cases, "teacher acceptance" is mandated by union contract provisions that require a faculty vote for strategies such as scheduling changes.

However, there is a difference between acceptance as demonstrated by signatures on a roster and buy-in that reflects the very way teachers and faculty work, think, and talk. Too often, principals mention a new reform effort at a faculty meeting and pass out some pamphlets, and when the faculty doesn't revolt, the principal assumes he or she has the active support of the staff. The term *buy-in* implies a business-type partnership in which the teacher is a willing, committed investor. True, meaningful buy-in to an instructional vision means that the faculty clearly understands what they are all working to achieve and what strategies they are going to use to do it. They use the same language in describing the school's vision, use common strategies to achieve it, and feel comfortable in the school's overall direction. Buy-in is most easily attained when the faculty have opportunity to jointly create the strategy and provide feedback, and when the vision adopted is one that they share. Regardless of the specific strategy used, it is hard to overstate the importance of helping the faculty buy into and share the overall instructional vision.

Focusing on scheduling, here are a few examples of how schools we have included in this book have jointly crafted strategic schedules:

- The Dever Elementary School created an action team to examine how to maximize time in the school. This team visited a school in New York City that was implementing an innovative schedule to accomplish the school's goals. The team found the visit very helpful because they were able to observe the strategy in action and thus better understand how and why it was effective. The action team also completed a resource review similar to that included in Chapter 8. The action team and the principal both discussed the site visit and the findings from the resource review with the entire staff and came up with five options for changing the schedule. After further discussion, the school chose to implement one of the proposed options on a one-week trial basis during the month of June. This proved to be a nonthreatening strategy for teachers and was essential for faculty buy-in. The teachers decided to adopt the new schedule permanently, and they worked with the committee to refine it for optimal efficiency. The schedule is now reviewed and refined each year.

- The Mather Elementary School also uses teacher input to help develop and implement its schedule. In designing the schedule, the principal took care to ensure it treated all students and teachers fairly. A key step in the process has been input of the teaching staff. Teacher input has been gathered in a number of ways, including year-end questionnaires, staff meetings focused on scheduling, and quick, informal consultations during the summer regarding the tentative schedule. Through these means, the principal learned that Mather teachers did not want their planning and development time scheduled as the first morning activity because the flow of morning teacher time is disrupted when students are immediately sent to specialist instruction on arrival at school. He also found that most teachers preferred their planning and development time to back up against their lunchtime. Allowing teacher teams to have input into scheduling decisions created support for the schedule. As a result of these various inputs, the schedule improves each year (Shields, 1999).

3. Set Measurable Indicators of Progress and Measure Them

As part of adopting a new strategic plan, it is essential to develop indicators that measure whether its components are actually helping you address their intended purposes. We recommend that you develop indicators that measure both implementation of the plan's components as well as concrete improvements you hope to see. Note that we are not suggesting that you develop an exhaustive system for evaluation that includes detailed metrics. Instead, create indicators that are concrete and will allow you to know whether the reforms are being implemented as intended, as well as those that help you measure student progress.

These indicators will vary depending on each school's goals, strategies, and resources. For example, indicators for measuring the impact of new blocks of common planning time might include the following:

- All teachers have one or more 90-minute blocks of time for collaboration each week.
- Teachers meet together to use the common planning time to review student work according to established rubrics and feel that the time is well spent. This could be measured informally or formally through periodic surveys or by active principal participation in the collaborative planning process.
- Weekly student assessments (as reviewed in collaborative planning time) indicate that all students are mastering material covered, or where they indicate otherwise, additional time is allotted to redress the issue for students who need more time or a different presentation style.
- The schedule adopted is supported by professional development and curriculum (e.g., in block schedules, teachers are regularly given tools and ideas for using longer blocks of instruction well and incorporating experiential learning activities).
- The schedule does not create problems with student discipline or teacher morale.

How often the leadership team reviews progress will depend on the goal. Whether teachers are using common planning time could be measured informally and formally every day or week. The results of the measurements could be discussed weekly, quarterly, or annually, depending on the priority placed on the use of planning time. Other goals might be checked only annually. As you measure progress, you may find that the chosen strategy has consequences and effects you hadn't considered that enhance or reduce the effectiveness of your plan. Depending on what you find, you should modify the strategy, provide additional support to teachers, or in some cases, defer implementation until you can create the preconditions that will allow you to succeed.

For example, one elementary school we worked with chose to reduce class size from 24 to 15 in Grades K through 3 by integrating all special-education resource room and ELL students and teachers into regular homeroom classes. This move added special-education and ELL teachers to homeroom classes, thus lowering overall class size for the entire day and allowing all students to benefit from these teachers' expertise and instruction. Some teachers found that the newly small class sizes let them understand individual student learning needs, create individual learning plans, work as partners with parents, and employ new instructional strategies. Other teachers felt unexpectedly overwhelmed. They weren't sure how to help students struggling with the reading *combined* with other learning challenges, and they weren't comfortable with small-group and differentiated instruction. Special-education-trained teachers who were expert in diagnosing and determining strategies to respond to individual needs struggled with classroom management issues even with a small group of 15.

Now, you may wonder whether the school conducted a sophisticated study or involved outsiders to help assess their implementation of small class sizes. In fact, they did nothing fancy. They simply made their reasons for moving to the new strategy very explicit and resolved to regularly review whether the new student grouping was working the way they envisioned to improve instruction. They asked whether reducing class size for all students to 15 was

- enabling teachers to spend time assessing and diagnosing individual student learning needs,
- enabling teachers to target attention in the priority subjects with the students who need it most,
- giving teachers more time to work as partners with parents,
- reducing classroom management challenges,
- enabling the implementation of individual attention strategies that larger class sizes didn't, and
- making teachers' lives more manageable and teaching more fun.

They made sure to include all teachers who were affected by the strategy in the evaluation process. The beauty of using this kind of process is that it reinforces the reasons for the structural change in the first place and enables creative thinking about what changes need to be made in the implementation of the strategy to make it more effective.

4. Adapt Your Strategic Plan Over Time, Flexibly Using Resources to Support Changing Situations

We have discussed the many ways that strategic school leaders challenge the "givens" of their existing school organization and design a new organization. They also adjust their design to match changing student needs and teacher capacity. An organizational design is not a static end result of a strategic planning process. It is a dynamic, living plan. We have found that high-performing school leaders continuously adjust their organizational design in response to student needs and changing teacher capacities and interests. They use their self-evaluation systems to monitor which strategies are working and which need to be revisited for improvement.

One school we worked with recently adopted a complete instructional design that included frequent teacher-administered assessment of reading skills, starting in the first grade. They adopted reading materials and lessons appropriate for the reading levels of the incoming students and incorporated small-group instruction and discussion into their instructional practice. Students in this school entered first grade with a wide range of reading fluency, with some already reading and others just beginning to connect letters to sounds. At the time of implementation, the first-grade teaching team had two brand-new teachers, one five-year teacher, and one veteran teacher. All of them were just learning to implement the new reading approach.

The principal realized that this combination of teacher skills would not ensure success for this vital first-grade cohort, so she adjusted her organization. First, she switched an outstanding second-grade teacher with one of the new first-grade teachers. Next, she directed additional expert resources to support the first-grade students and teachers by "cashing in" a librarian position to fund a full-time literacy coach/reading instructor. She also freed the special-education resource room teacher to work with the first-grade team during their literacy period each day and during their weekly planning time so that the resource support provided would be integrated with the first-grade curriculum. She charged this six-person team (three experts and three relative novices) with collective responsibility for the reading attainment of the 94 first-grade students, and they responded admirably, meeting the school's ambitious goals.

As this example illustrates, organizational strategies are dynamic. They can and must evolve as teacher capacity and student needs shift over time. As your teaching team becomes increasingly expert, you can shift coaching resources elsewhere, or you can distribute teacher expertise across other teacher teams. Linda Nathan (2001), headmaster of the Boston Arts Academy (BAA) high school, summarized the idea of strategically adapting organizations to student and teacher needs over time in this description of her school's process for creating the master schedule:

No single school schedule can satisfy every need. Every choice in the making of a schedule involves trade-offs. Moreover, the life of a school is dynamic, not static. Since BAA's birth four years ago, we have had four different schedules. These changes reflect our growth as a school (from 160 to 400 students) as well as changing priorities. (p. 2)

Strategic schools are learning organizations. They reflect their learning in their organizational strategies by tinkering with them constantly.

Redefining Systems and Policies to Support Strategic Schools

11

Throughout this book, we have provided research and advice on how individual schools can use resources strategically. Designing strategic school organizations that improve student performance is a worthy goal, but it is not our hope to lift a few schools to excellence in a system that pulls most schools toward mediocrity. To succeed in preparing all children to participate in the technologically advanced twenty-first century, we will have to go beyond creating a few strategic schools and instead find ways to create whole systems of them.

Despite the importance of system reform, until now, we have hardly touched on the vital role that school systems (whether public school districts or charter networks) play in fostering excellence. We begin with a school-level vision because district leaders, reformers, and policy makers can only design effective systems, structures, and policies when they are clear about what they are trying to enable within schools. True systemic support demands change in system-level policies, strategies, and belief systems—moving from a top-down, mandate-driven organization to one that exists to solve problems and support and supervise school leaders in making strong resource decisions that will support their school designs and their students' particular needs. It requires us to rethink the type of leadership skills school principals need and the way we allocate people, time, and money to schools. Systemic change demands that we overcome the institutional inertia that shackles creativity by making resources more flexible. It requires school systems to better support principal decision making and to create new ways for measuring resource use and holding schools accountable.

We close by reviewing the guiding resource principles that we have discussed in this book and highlighting the critical support that schools need to implement them more effectively as well as systemic barriers they currently face in doing so. From this analysis, we derive a set of priority areas for system redesign and policy action that would enable strategic schools to become more of the norm.

PRACTICES AND POLICIES THAT SUPPORT AND THWART STRATEGIC SCHOOLS

Figure 11.1 describes the kinds of support strategic schools need from school systems or other providers to implement the guiding resource principles, as well as barriers schools face in trying to implement each of them. Looking first at the strategy area of teaching quality, the figure highlights numerous ways a school system might support schools in attracting, developing, and retaining the best teachers. A strategic school system would actively work to increase the size and quality of its teaching pool and seek to match the needs of schools in more nuanced ways. Such a school district would not leave the design of expert coaching models and recruitment of coaches to schools, but neither would it mandate that each school use the same kind of coaches and indiscriminately assign them to each school. Instead, a strategic system would identify or develop several different coaching models that fit different kinds of school needs and work to recruit a pool of coaches that schools could choose from to fit the specific personalities and needs of the school staff and students. Strategic schools in some school systems face particular challenges in finding ways to reward their best teachers financially because the current salary systems reward experience and course-taking rather than demonstrated classroom proficiency or leadership responsibilities. School systems that worked to restructure salary structures to keep the best teachers would give strategic schools a huge advantage.

Turning next to the "Individual Attention" strategy area, perhaps the most important support schools need is powerful assessment tools that align with their instructional model and state standards. As shown in Figure 11.1, assessment is a particular area in which individual school development can be time consuming and expensive. Despite this, schools operate with a patchwork set of assessment tools that vary from school to school. Worse still are assessment protocols that conflict with the curriculum order or goals of the school. These drain valuable time and create distractions and frustration for schools that may be implementing very

Figure 11.1 Practices and policies that support and thwart strategic schools

Guiding Resource Principle	What Strategic Schools Need From School Systems or Other Providers	Current Barriers
Teaching Quality		
Hiring and organizing staff to fit school needs in terms of expertise, philosophy, and schedule	• Pool of high-quality candidates that fit school needs	• Lack of control in hiring and assignment • Limited availability of highly flexible teachers who can work part-time or have multiple certifications
Integrating significant resources for well-designed professional development (PD) that provides expert support to implement the school's core instructional design	• PD resources organized to promote school's strategic design and specific needs	• Fragmented, unstrategic district PD offerings that don't align with school needs
Designing teacher work schedules to include blocks of collaborative planning time effectively used to improve classroom practice	• Support creating schedules that provide significant time for teachers to work collaboratively	• Contracts that limit the total amount and restrict the use of teacher time
Enacting systems that promote individual teacher growth through induction, leadership opportunities, PD planning, evaluation, and compensation	• Induction and leadership development support that integrates with school-level resources and approach • Career ladders and evaluation and compensation systems that attract, develop, and retain the best teachers	• Limited new-teacher support not matched to school or teacher needs • Funding systems that charge schools for average teacher salaries even when teachers are new, limiting school-level resources for new-teacher support • Career structures and evaluation and compensation systems that reward longevity instead of leadership or expertise

(Continued)

Figure 11.1 (Continued)

Guiding Resource Principle	What Strategic Schools Need From School Systems or Other Providers	Current Barriers
Individual Attention and Personal Learning Environments		
Assessing student learning to adjust instruction and support	• Aligned assessment tools that help diagnose learning needs	• Assessment requirements that don't provide information to guide instruction or don't match instruction
Creating smaller group sizes and reduced teacher loads in high-need areas	• District-specific models for effective ways of organizing to support individual learning needs in content as well as program areas like special education and bilingual education	• Union contracts and state regulations that mandate class sizes by grade and subject. • Teacher certification restrictions that limit interdisciplinary instruction and flexible grouping
Organizing structures that foster personal relationships between students and teachers	• District-specific models for effective ways of organizing smaller schools and communities	• Large schools that make it hard to create a sense of community
Strategic Use of Student Time Emphasizing Core Academics and Literacies		
Maximizing time, including longer blocks of uninterrupted time, that students spend on academic subjects	• District-specific models for strategic schedules that fit state, school district, and union time requirements	• Union contracts that limit the way time can be structured • Short student and teacher workdays and work-years in some districts and states
Varying time and instructional programs to ensure all students meet rigorous academic standards	• District-specific models for varying time and additional resources when needed	• Freedom from rigid grade structures and course requirements

effective models that do not align. Furthermore, while we have described a variety of models for providing individual attention to students such as tutoring, selected small class sizes, and flexible grouping, there is much to be learned in this area. While school systems often specify class sizes and caseloads for categories of special-needs and English-Language-Learning students, few provide or promote powerful models for organizing students and teachers more effectively to learn specific kinds of skills. Schools need help creating a toolkit of effective organizational strategies as well as instructional ones.

Finally, to make effective use of student time, schools can use assistance in creating effective school schedules that maximize the use of time and fit teacher- and student-level needs. In some school systems, too little time exists either because of the state context or union contracts. In our work, we have seen wide variation in the amount of instructional time available across districts.

CRITICAL AREAS FOR SYSTEM AND POLICY REDESIGN

While there are specific strategies and actions districts can take to support each guiding resource principle, the overarching concept of strategic schools is that it's not any one specific input, but the *combination* of resource strategies that has to match changing and subtly varying school needs. This moves the model for supporting, supervising, and even funding schools from defining specific inputs and actions to finding ways to make resources more flexible and their use more strategic (McLaughlin & Talbert, 2003; Miles, 2006; Miles & Roza, 2005; Spillane, 1996). This paradigm shift suggests that districts and policy makers can promote more strategic schools by working in six key areas:

1. Build principal capacity to manage resources strategically.

2. Identify and replicate selected high-performance designs and strategies that fit the district's budget, human resource capacity, and regulatory and contractual context.

3. Change the way districts conduct and organize school planning, supervision, and support to encourage the use of people, time, and money in high-performance ways that fit school needs.

4. Revise funding systems to ensure equity across schools and empower school leaders to use resources more flexibly.

5. Revise district practices, state policies, and union contract provisions that limit hiring discretion, class size, and scheduling flexibility.

6. Create a high-quality pool of teachers that meets evolving school-level needs in subject area and expertise.

CONCLUSION

In the beginning of this book, we suggested that educators dream of changing lives through connecting with students around learning. We acknowledged that it isn't often that school leaders link school budgets and resources with good dreams; more likely, they have budget nightmares. We hope that the frameworks, strategies, and tools presented in these pages provide ways of connecting your dreams and goals for students with specific ways of organizing and allocating resources. While the field of education already has a strong research base around the practices and characteristics of excellent schools, there has been less clarity around effective resource use. Nationwide, practitioners and researchers continue to use blunt ways to support and measure resource use in schools.

In this chapter, we turned to the vital topic of ways that school systems and policies must be redesigned to better support effective resource organization. We highlighted the complex web of challenges that confront those trying to create strategic schools in most states and in most districts. This web can entangle even the most intrepid school leader and can lead to discouragement and a stagnant reform cycle in which partially implemented ideas are thrown away and replaced by other good ideas, which are only partially implemented.

Each day we see school leaders succeed despite these odds. They do this by identifying their most pressing student needs and aligning all available people, time, and money to purposefully address them. They summon the courage to pursue their instructional vision despite systemic and cultural barriers, and they use relentless persistence to find a way to turn these everyday resources into powerful tools to achieve student success.

References

Allegretto, S., Corcoran, S., & Mishel, L. (2004). *How does teacher pay compare?* Washington, DC: Economic Policy Institute.

Allington, R., & Cunningham, P. (2002). *Schools that work: Where all children read and write.* Boston: Allyn & Bacon.

Archibald, S. (2001). *A case study of dramatic resource reallocation to improve student achievement: Harrison Place High School.* Madison: Consortium for Policy Research in Education Working Paper, University of Wisconsin–Madison.

Berliner, D. (1979). *Research on teaching: Concepts, findings and implications.* Berkeley, CA: McCutchan.

Black, P., & Wiliam, D. (1998). Assessment and classroom learning. *Assessment in Education, 5*(1), 7–74.

Bodilly, S. (1998). *Lessons from New American Schools' scale-up phase.* Santa Monica, CA: RAND.

Boston Plan for Excellence. (2002). *Boston Plan for Excellence contract for coaches.* Boston: Author.

Boston Plan for Excellence. (2003). *Guide to implementing collaborative coaching model.* Boston: Author.

Bransford, J., Brown, A., & Cocking, R. (Eds.). (1999). *How people learn.* Washington, DC: National Academy Press.

Carlisle, J., Litt, J., & Shields, R. (2006). *What makes schools work? Notable practices in two high-performing schools.* Rochester, NY: Rochester City School District.

Carpenter, T. P., Fennema, E., Peterson, P., Chiang, C., & Loef, M. (1989). Using knowledge of children's mathematics thinking in classroom teaching: An experimental study. *American Journal of Education Research, 26,* 499–531.

Center for Collaborative Education. (2001). *How Boston pilot schools use freedom over budget, staffing, and scheduling to meet student needs.* Boston: Author.

Cohen, D., & Hill, H. (2000). Instructional policy and classroom performance: The mathematics reform in California. *Teachers College Record, 102*(4), 9–26.

Darling-Hammond, L. (2001). *The right to learn: A blueprint for creating schools that work.* San Francisco: Jossey-Bass.

Deuel, L., & Stoyco, L. (1999). Block scheduling in large, urban high schools: Effects on academic achievement, student behavior, and staff perceptions. *High School Journal, 83*(1), 4–25.

Edmonds, R. (1979). *A discussion of the literature and issues related to effective schooling.* Cambridge, MA: Center for Urban Studies, Harvard Graduate School of Education.

Education Resource Strategies. (2006). [Average time in school]. Unpublished raw data.

Education Resource Strategies & Annenberg Institute for School Reform at Brown University. (2004, September). *Becoming a capable and accountable system: A review of professional development and curriculum in the Baltimore City Public School system.* Retrieved December 28, 2007, from http://www.educationre sourcestrategies.org/pdfs/baltimore_pd.pdf

Education Trust. (1999). *Dispelling the myth: High poverty schools exceeding expectations.* Washington, DC: Author.

EdWeek. (2007). *Class size: Research center.* Retrieved September 20, 2007, from http://www.edweek.org/rc/issues/class-size/

Elmore, R. (2002). *Bridging the gap between standards and achievement: The imperative for professional development in education.* New York: Albert Shanker Institute.

Elmore, R., & Burney, D. (1999). Investing in teacher learning: Staff development and instructional improvement. In L. Darling-Hammond & G. Sykes (Eds.), *Teaching as the learning profession: Handbook of policy and practice* (pp. 263–291). San Francisco: Jossey-Bass.

Elmore, R., Peterson, P., & McCarthey, S. (1996). *Restructuring in the classroom: Teaching, learning, & school organization.* San Francisco: Jossey-Bass.

Finn, J., Gerber, S., Achilles, C., & Boyd-Zaharias, J. (2001). The enduring effects of small classes. *Teachers College Record, 103,* 145–183.

French, D., Atkinson, M., & Rugen, L. (2007). *Creating small schools: A handbook for raising equity and achievement.* Thousand Oaks, CA: Corwin Press.

Fullan, M. (1993). Why teachers must become change agents. *Educational Leadership, 50*(6), 12–17.

Glennan, T. (1998). *New American schools after six years.* Washington, DC: RAND.

Goodlad, J. (1984). *A place called school.* New York: McGraw-Hill.

Greenwald, R., Hedges, L., & Laine, R. (1996). The effect of school resources on student achievement. *Review of Educational Research, 66,* 361–396.

Gruber, C., & Onwuegbuzie, A. J. (2001). Effects of block scheduling on academic achievement among high school students. *High School Journal, 84*(4), 32–42.

Halbach, A., Ehrle, K., Zahorick, J., & Molnar, A. (2001). Class size reduction: From promise to practice. *Educational Leadership, 58*(6), 32–35.

Hanushek, E. (1997). Assessing the effects of school resources on student performance: An update. *Education Evaluation and Policy Analysis, 19,* 141–164.

Hargreaves, A. (1994). *Changing teachers, changing times: Teachers' work and culture in the postmodern age.* New York: Teachers College Press.

Hawley, W. D. (2002). *The keys to effective schools.* Thousand Oaks, CA: Corwin Press.

Hawley, W. D., & Valli, L. (2007). Design principles for learner-centered professional development. In W. D. Hawley & D. Rollie (Eds.), *The keys to effective schools: Educational reform as school improvement* (2nd ed., pp. 117–138). Thousand Oaks, CA: Corwin Press.

Hedges, L., Laine, R., & Greenwald, R. (1994). Does money matter: A meta-analysis of studies of the effects of differential school inputs on student outcomes. *Educational Researcher, 23*(3), 5–14.

Holland, H. (2005). Teaching teachers: Professional development to improve student achievement. *American Educational Research Association Research Points, 3*(1), 1–4.

Ingersoll, R. (1999). The problem of underqualified teachers in American secondary schools. *Educational Researcher, 28*(2), 26–37.

Ingersoll, R. M., & Smith, T. M. (2004, March). Do teacher induction and mentoring matter? *NASSP Bulletin, 88*, 638.

Jacob, B., & Lefgren, L. (2006, Spring). When principals rate teachers. *Education Next*, pp. 59–64.

Jenkins, E., Queen, A., & Algozzine, L. (2002). To block or not to block: That's not the question. *Journal of Education Research, 95*(4), 196–202.

Johnson, S. (2007). *Finders keepers: Helping new teachers survive and thrive in our schools.* San Francisco: Jossey-Bass.

Keller, B. (2006, November 8). More teacher-incentive grants trickle out. *EdWeek,* p. 14.

Knapp, M., McCaffrey, T., & Swanson, J. (2003, April 21–25). *District support for professional learning: What research says and has yet to establish.* Paper presented at the Annual Meeting of the American Educational Research Association, Chicago.

Ladd, H., & Hansen, J. (1999). *Making money matter: Financing America's schools.* Washington, DC: National Academy Press.

Lawrence, W., & McPherson, D. (2002). A comparative study of block scheduling and traditional scheduling on academic achievement. *Journal of Instructional Psychology, 27*(3), 178–182.

Lee, V., & Smith, J. (1995). Effects of high school restructuring and size on gains in achievement and engagement for early secondary school students. *Sociology of Education, 68*, 241–270.

Lee, V., & Smith, J. (1996). Collective responsibility for learning and its effects on gains in achievement for early secondary school students. *American Journal of Education, 104*, 103–147.

Lee, V., Smith, J., & Croninger, R. (1997). How high school organization influences the equitable distribution of learning in mathematics and science. *Sociology of Education, 70*, 128–150.

Levin, H. (1991). *Accelerating the progress of all students* (Special report No. 31). Albany: Nelson A. Rockefeller Institute of Government, State University of New York.

Loveless, T. (1998). *The tracking and ability grouping debate.* Retrieved December 28, 2007, from www.edexcellence.net/foundation/publication/publication .cfm?id=127

Marchant, G., & Paulson, S. (2001). Differential school functioning in a block schedule: A comparison of academic profiles. *High School Journal, 84*(4), 12–20.

Marzano, R. (2003). *What works in schools: Translating research into action.* Alexandria, VA: Association for Supervision and Curriculum Development.

May, H., Supovitz, J., & Perda, D. (2004). *A longitudinal study of the impact of America's Choice on student performance in Rochester, New York, 1998–2003.* Philadelphia: Consortium for Policy Research in Education, University of Pennsylvania Graduate School of Education.

McLaughlin, M., & Talbert, J. (2003). *Reforming districts: How districts support reform* (Document R-03-6). Seattle: University of Washington, Center for the Study of Teaching Policy.

McLaughlin, M., & Talbert, J. (2005). *Developing the teaching profession: Learning to improve student achievement.* New York: Teachers College Press.

Meir, D. (1992, Summer). Reinventing teaching. *Teachers College Record, 93,* 594–609.

Miles, K., & Darling-Hammond, L. (1997). Rethinking the reallocation of teaching resources: Some lessons from high-performing schools. In *CPRE Research Report No. RR-38.* Philadelphia: Consortium for Policy Research in Education.

Miles, K., & Darling-Hammond, L. (1998). Rethinking the allocation of teaching resources: Some lessons from high performing schools. *Educational Evaluation and Policy Analysis, 20*(1), 9–29.

Miles, K., & Frank, S. (2006). *A strategic review of district and school resources in Chicago Public Schools 2005–2006.* Watertown, MA: Education Resource Strategies.

Miles, K., Shields, R., & City, E. (2007). *The cost of small high schools: A literature review.* Watertown, MA: Education Resource Strategies. Retrieved September 12, 2007, from http://www.educationresourcestrategies.org

Miles, K. H. (1997). *Spending more at the edges.* Unpublished dissertation, Graduate School of Education, Harvard University.

Miles, K. H. (2001). *Rethinking school resources.* Alexandria, VA: New American Schools.

Miles, K. H. (2006). *Rethinking school-system resources to create excellence and equity.* Providence, RI: Annenberg Institute of School Reform.

Miles, K. H., & Roza, M. (2005, Winter). Using weighted student formula as a means to greater equity. *Peabody Journal of Education, 81*(3), 39–62.

Mishel, L., & Rothstein, R. (2002). *The class size debate.* Washington, DC: Economic Policy Institute.

Moir, E. (2003, July). *Launching the next generation of teachers through quality induction.* Paper prepared for the National Commission on Teaching and America's Future State Partners' Symposium, Denver, CO.

Mosteller, F. (1995). The Tennessee study of class size in the early school grades. *Future of Children, 5,* 113–127.

Murnane, R. (1991). Interpreting the evidence on "Does Money Matter?" *Harvard Journal on Legislation, 28,* 457–465.

Murnane, R., & Levy, F. (1996). *Teaching the new basic skills.* New York: Free Press.

Murphy, C. (1997). Finding time for faculties to study together. *Journal of Staff Development, 18*(3), 29–32.

Murphy, J. (2004). *Leadership for literacy.* Thousand Oaks, CA: Corwin Press.

Nathan, L. (2001). *The Boston Arts Academy schedule: Form follows function.* Unpublished manuscript.

National Association of Secondary School Principals. (2004). *Breaking Ranks II: Strategies for leading high school reform.* Reston, VA: Author.

National Education Association. (1990). *Tracing the evolution of KEYS.* Washington DC: Author. Retrieved December 28, 2007, from http://www.nea.org/school quality/history-keys.html

National Education Commission on Time and Learning. (1994). *Prisoners of time.* Retrieved December 23, 2007, from http://www.ed.gov/pubs/PrisonersOfTime/ Prisoners.html

National Institute for Excellence in Teaching. (2005). *Understanding the Teacher Advancement Program.* Washington, DC: Author.

Nelson, G., & Landel, C. (2006). A collaborative approach for elementary science. *Educational Leadership, 64*(4), 72–75.

Neufeld, B., & Roper, D. (2003). *Coaching as a strategy for instructional capacity development: Promises and practicalities.* Washington, DC: Aspen Institute.

Newmann, F., & Associates. (1996). *Authentic achievement: Restructuring schools for intellectual quality.* San Francisco: Jossey-Bass.

Newmann, F., Smith, B., Allensworth, E., & Bryk, A. S. (2001). *School instructional program coherence: Benefits and challenges.* Chicago: Chicago Consortium on School Research.

Oakes, J. (1989). Detracking schools: Early lessons from the field. *Phi Delta Kappan, 73,* 448–454.

Odden, A., & Archibald, S. (2001). *Reallocating resources: How to boost student achievement without asking for more.* Thousand Oaks, CA: Corwin Press.

Odden, A., Picus, L., Goetz, M., & Fermanich, M. (2006, June 30). *An evidence-based approach to school finance adequacy in Washington.* Hollywood, CA: Lawrence O. Picus and Associates.

Osofsky, D., Sinner, G., & Wolk, D. (2003). *Changing systems to personalize learning: The power of advisories.* Providence, RI: Education Alliance at Brown University.

Raywid, M. A. (1993). Finding time for collaboration. *Educational Leadership, 51*(1), 30–34.

Rice, J. (2002a, November). Some guidelines for investing in class size reduction. *Leads,* pp. 1–2. Retrieved December 28, 2007, from http://www.education .umd.edu/EDPL/CEPAL/Leads/November2002.pdf

Rice, J. K. (2002b). Some guidelines for investing in class size reduction. *Leads,* pp. 1–2. Retrieved January 14, 2008, from http://education.umd.edu/EDPA/ CEPAL/pdf/publications/LEADS%20Fall%202002.pdf

Rice, J. K., Croninger, R. G., & Roellke, C. (2002). The effects of block scheduling high school mathematics courses on student achievement and teachers' use of time: Implications for educational productivity. *Economics of Education Review, 21,* 599–607.

Rivkin, S., Hanushek, E., & Kain, J. (2000). *Teachers, schools and academic achievement* (Working Paper No. 6691). Cambridge, MA: National Bureau of Economic Research.

Rivkin, S., Hanushek, E., & Kain, J. (2002). *Teachers, schools and academic achievement.* Dallas: University of Texas–Dallas, Texas Schools Project.

Roth, J., Brooks-Gunn, J., Linver, M., & Hofferth, S. (2003). What happens during the school day? Time diaries from a national sample of elementary school teachers. *Teachers College Record, 106,* 317–343.

Rothstein, R. (1996). *Where's the money going? Changes in the level and composition of education spending, 1991–96.* Washington, DC: Economic Policy Institute.

Rothstein, R., & Miles, K. (1995). *Where's the money gone? Changes in the level and composition of education spending.* Washington, DC: Economic Policy Institute.

Rowan, B., Chiang, F. S., & Miller, R. J. (1997). Using research on employees' performance to study the effects of teachers on students' achievement. *Sociology of Education, 70,* 256–284.

Sarason, S. (1971/1982). *The culture of the school and the problem of change.* Boston: Allyn & Bacon.

Schmidt, W., McKnight, C., & Raizen, S. (1996). *A splintered vision: An investigation of U.S. science and mathematics education* (Executive Summary). East Lansing: Michigan State University.

Sheerens, J., & Bosker, R. (1997). *The foundations of educational effectiveness.* Oxford, UK: Elsevier Science.

Shields, R. (1999). *Five case studies on revising school schedules.* Alexandria, VA: New American Schools.

Shields, R., & Miles, K. (2008). *Strategic designs: Lessons from leading edge small urban high schools.* Watertown, MA: Education Resource Strategies and Gates Foundation.

Silva, E. (2007). *On the clock: Rethinking the way schools use time.* Washington, DC: Education Sector.

Sizer, T. R. (1992). *Horace's compromise: The dilemma of the American high school.* Boston: Houghton Mifflin.

Slavin, R. E. (1995). Detracking and its detractors: Flawed evidence, flawed values. *Phi Delta Kappan, 77,* 220–223.

Smith, B. (1998). *It's about time: Opportunities to learn in Chicago's elementary schools.* Chicago: Consortium on Chicago School Research.

Spillane, J. (1996). School districts matter: Local educational authorities and state instructional policy. *Educational Policy, 10*(1), 63–87.

Springboard Schools. (2003). *After the test: How schools are using data to close the achievement gap.* San Francisco: Author.

Stigler, J., & Hiebert, J. (1999). *The teaching gap: Best ideas from the world's teachers improving education in the classroom.* New York: Free Press.

Supovitz, J., & Corcoran, T. (2000). *Evaluating standards in practice in Cincinnati public schools.* Philadelphia: Consortium of Policy Research in Education, University of Philadelphia.

Swaim, M., & Swaim, S. (1999, Fall). Teacher time. *American Educator.*

Taylor, B. M., & Taxis, H. (1999). *Translating characteristics of effective school reading programs into practice.* Retrieved December 28, 2007, from http://www.ciera.org/library/presos/2000/2000-CSI/btaylor/csi-taylor taxis.pdf

Time, Learning, and Afterschool Task Force. (2007). *A new day for learning.* Retrieved December 23, 2007, from http://www.edutopia.org/pdfs/ANewDay forLearning.pdf

Trenta, L., & Newman, I. (2002). A four year longitudinal study of the effects of block scheduling on student outcome variables. *American Secondary Education, 31*(1), 54–71.

Tyack, D., & Cuban, L. (1995). *Tinkering toward utopia: A century of public school reform.* Cambridge, MA: Harvard University Press.

Tyack, D., & Tobin, W. (1994). The "grammar" of schooling: Why has it been so hard to change? *American Educational Research Journal, 31,* 453–479.

U.S. Department of Education, National Center for Education Statistics. (1997). *Digest of education statistics* (Table 64). Washington, DC: Author.

U.S. Department of Education, National Center for Education Statistics. (1999a). *Digest of education statistics* (Tables 90 and 93). Washington, DC: Author.

U.S. Department of Education, National Center for Education Statistics. (1999b). *Digest of education statistics* (Tables 168 and 170). Washington, DC: Author.

U.S. Department of Education, National Center for Education Statistics. (2003). *Data from the U.S. Department of Education, NCES, National Assessment of Educational Progress (NAEP), 2003 Reading Assessment Table 9.1, and 2002 Writing Assessment, Table 10.1.A.* Washington, DC: Author.

Veal, W., & Flinders, D. (2001). How block scheduling reform affects classroom practice. *High School Journal, 84*(4), 21–31.

Wasik, B., & Slavin, R. E. (1993). Preventing early reading failure with one-to-one tutoring: A review of five programs. *Reading Research Quarterly, 28,* 178–200.

Weerasinghe, D., & Anderson, M. (2001). *Validation studies and post-hoc analysis of classroom effectiveness indices.* Dallas, TX: Dallas Independent School District.

Weller, D., & McLeskey, J. (2000). Block scheduling and inclusion in a high school: Teacher perceptions of the benefits and challenges. *Remedial and Special Education, 21*(4), 209–219.

Wenglinsky, H., & Silverstein, S. (2006). The science training teachers need. *Educational Leadership, 64*(4), 24–29.

WestEd. (1998, April 20). *Research report on time.* Paper presented at the PACE Media/Education Writers Seminar, San Francisco.

Williams, T., Kirst, M., Haertel, E., et al. (2005). *Similar students, different results: Why do some schools do better? A large-scale survey of California elementary schools serving low-income students.* Mountain View, CA: EdSource. Retrieved January 15, 2008, from http://edsourceonline.org/pdf/SimStu05.pdf

Word, E., Johnson, J., & Bain, H. (1990). *Student/Teacher Achievement Ratio (STAR): Tennessee's K–3 class size study: Final summary report 1985–1990.* Nashville: Tennessee State University, Center of Excellence for Research in Basic Skills.

Zapeda, S., & Mayers, R. (2001). New kids on the block schedule: Beginning teachers face challenges. *High School Journal, 84*(4), 1–11.

Zurawski, C. (2003). Class size: Counting students can count. *American Educational Research Association Research Points, 1*(2), 1–4.

Index

CORWIN PRESS

The Corwin Press logo—a raven striding across an open book—represents the union of courage and learning. Corwin Press is committed to improving education for all learners by publishing books and other professional development resources for those serving the field of PreK–12 education. By providing practical, hands-on materials, Corwin Press continues to carry out the promise of its motto: **"Helping Educators Do Their Work Better."**

AMERICAN ASSOCIATION OF SCHOOL ADMINISTRATORS

The American Association of School Administrators, founded in 1865, is the professional organization for more than 13,000 educational leaders across the United States. AASA's mission is to support and develop effective school system leaders who are dedicated to the highest quality public education for all children. For more information, visit www.aasa.org.

NATIONAL ASSOCIATION OF SECONDARY SCHOOL

PRINCIPALS

Promoting Excellence in School Leadership

The National Association of Secondary School Principals—promoting excellence in school leadership since 1916—provides its members the professional resources to serve as visionary leaders. NASSP further promotes student leadership development through its sponsorship of the National Honor Society®, the National Junior Honor Society®, and the National Association of Student Councils®. For more information, visit www.principals.org.